NATURAL
ENEMY

AN ORIGINAL NOVEL OF THE MARVEL UNIVERSE

ANT-MAN

NATURAL ENEMY

AN ORIGINAL NOVEL OF THE MARVEL UNIVERSE

JASON STARR

ANT-MAN: NATURAL ENEMY. Published by MARVEL WORLDWIDE, INC., a subsidiary of MARVEL ENTERTAINMENT, LLC. OFFICE OF PUBLICATION: 135 West 50th Street, New York, NY 10020. Copyright © 2015 MARVEL

ISBN# 978-0-7851-9323-4

Printed in the U.S.A.

ALAN FINE, President, Marvel Entertainment; DAN BUCKLEY, President, TV, Publishing and Brand Management; JOE QUESADA, Chief Creative Officer; TOM BREVOORT, SVP of Publishing; DAVID BOGART, SVP of Operations & Procurement, Publishing; C.B. CEBULSKI, VP of International Development & Brand Management; DAVID GABRIEL, SVP Print, Sales & Marketing; JIM O'KEEFE, VP of Operations & Logistics; DAN CARR, Executive Director of Publishing Technology; SUSAN CRESPI, Editorial Operations Manager; ALEX MORALES, Publishing Operations Manager; STAN LEE, Chairman Emeritus. For information regarding advertising in Marvel Comics or on Marvel. com, please contact Jonathan Rheingold, VP of Custom Solutions & Ad Sales, at jrheingold@ marvel.com. For Marvel subscription inquiries, please call 800-217-9158. **Manufactured between 4/10/2015 and 5/18/2015 by SHERIDAN BOOKS, INC., CHELSEA, MI, USA.**

First printing 2015
10 9 8 7 6 5 4 3 2 1

FRONT COVER ART BY
MIKE DEODATO & FRANK MARTIN

BACK COVER ART BY
RAMON ROSANAS & JORDAN BOYD

ANT-MAN CREATED BY STAN LEE, LARRY LIEBER & JACK KIRBY

Stuart Moore, Editor
Interior Design by Amanda Scurti
Front Cover Design by Nelson Ribeiro
Jacket and Casing Design by Joe Frontirre

Senior Editor, Special Projects: Jeff Youngquist
Assistant Editor: Sarah Brunstad
SVP Print, Sales & Marketing: David Gabriel
Editor In Chief: Axel Alonso
Chief Creative Officer: Joe Quesada
Publisher: Dan Buckley
Executive Producer: Alan Fine

For Chynna Skye Starr

ANT-MAN

NATURAL ENEMY

AN ORIGINAL NOVEL OF THE MARVEL UNIVERSE

JASON STARR

"The world flatters the elephant and tramples on the ant."
— Indian proverb

PROLOGUE

WILLIE DUGAN was crawling in the dark tunnel—on his way to escaping from Attica State Prison in upstate New York, where he'd been holed up for nine years—when Keith, one of the guys busting out with him, said, "I'm stuck, bro."

"What?" Willie had heard him—just didn't want to believe it.

"I said I'm stuck," Keith said. "I can't move at all."

"Try, man," Willie said.

"I *am* trying, bro. I can't move. I can't, I can't."

Willie tried to push him forward, but it was so cramped in the tunnel that he couldn't get much leverage. Something had to have happened to the roof; it must've caved in. Keith was a big guy—six-two, maybe two-twenty—but he wasn't fat. He should've fit through the tunnel easy.

"You gotta move," Willie said. "Dig into the ground, make more space."

"Tryin', bro. But the ground's like steel here."

"Try harder."

Willie counted to ten in his head, trying not to panic or think of worst-case scenarios. Then he said, "Okay, try again."

"I still can't move, Willie." Keith sounded like he was crying.

"I'm sorry, bro, I'm sorry."

"Just shut up and try," Willie said.

"I can't. I can't, man, I can't."

"Try, goddamn it." Willie summoned up all his strength to push. "Move, come on, dig!" he kept saying, but Keith didn't budge.

Now the worst-case scenario was hitting Willie. There wasn't much air in the tunnel, especially with Keith clogging it up, so there was a chance Willie would suffocate to death. Or worse: What if they found him here alive and dragged him back to prison? They'd put him in max solitary for organizing the break, and he'd have zero chance of ever getting out.

This was it, his one chance—do or die. If he didn't escape tonight, his life would be over; he'd die in jail an old man, unless he figured out a way to kill himself.

Yeah, if they brought him back alive, suicide would definitely be his only way out.

Willie tried to shove Keith again. Then Willie felt something hit his head—a chunk of dirt from the roof of the tunnel.

Keith said the words that could've been Willie's own thoughts: "It's caving, it's caving!"

Was this how Willie was going to die? God's last laugh? Given the choice between getting buried alive or going back to jail, Willie would've taken buried alive. But he wasn't planning to have to choose either of those options yet.

He hadn't spent nine years on that tunnel—all that planning, all that work—to go down like this. He used all his strength to somehow shove Keith forward.

"Go! Faster!" Willie shouted.

The tunnel was crumbling; there must've been an inch of dirt on his head. Willie had no idea how much farther they had to go. If they were a minute away, maybe they had a chance. Maybe. The tunnel was caving so fast now, he could hear it, like the beginning of an avalanche. Then the crash came, behind him, where Keith had been stuck just moments earlier. They'd be buried now if they'd stayed there, but Willie wasn't thinking about that. He was just thinking about moving ahead, getting out of the darkness.

"Faster!" he shouted again. "Come on!"

There was more crashing behind them. The whole tunnel was caving now. There was dirt everywhere—all over his body, in his mouth, in his eyes. And then he felt the ground beneath him begin sloping upward.

He kept clawing at the dirt. If he could still claw, that meant he was still alive.

And then, as the tunnel collapsed, he felt something different— grass, actual grass. The hole was about four feet wide, a bigger version of a groundhog's hole. His hands slipped on the dew a couple of times, but finally he was able to hoist himself up and out. He ignored the stinging in his eyes and saw light: It was coming from a lamppost, maybe fifty yards away. He didn't stop to marvel over his close call. Although his body was stiff as hell and he could barely see in front of him, he knew he couldn't waste any time. He spotted Keith and the other three guys scattering ahead of him, and he took his pre-planned route: He ran along the road for about a quarter mile, then made a left down a narrow street and a right two blocks later. Finally he reached the corner and waited.

Two minutes later, he saw the headlights of a car approaching, right on schedule. After the near-disaster in the tunnel, everything was working out. He had plenty of money put away—money he could live on for the rest of his life. It would be about five hours till wakeup time, when the guards would find out about the break. He had time to get to Canada, then use a fake Canadian passport to fly to Belize, then Kuwait, and then to that island in the South Pacific.

He could do all this, but he wouldn't. He'd spent too much energy over the past nine years dreaming about this day. Freedom was great, but there was one thing that would make everything right, that would give him real happiness.

Yeah, it was time to get some payback.

ONE

ANTHONY HAWKINS, twenty-two years old, in a black ski mask with one wide slit for his eyes, entered the bodega on Third Avenue and 128th Street, took out his piece—a nine-millimeter Glock, same gun he'd used during his entire spree of holdups in the New York City area—aimed it at the old guy behind the counter, and said, "Give it up, yo."

"Come on, kid," the guy—Spanish accent, sounding tired—said. "You ain't gonna get rich off me."

Anthony noticed the camera, aiming right at him from the corner near the door. He shot at it, missed. He shot again, hit it this time, and the camera shattered.

A woman in the back—he didn't know anybody else was in the store—screamed.

Anthony, nervous, shouted down the aisle, "Hey, you come out here now!"

The scared, crying Asian lady walked toward the front of the store with her hands up. Then Anthony thought he saw the old man reach for something behind the counter—maybe a gun.

Anthony aimed the Glock at him and yelled, "The register! Clean it out right now, or I'll kill both of you, I swear I will!"

Then Anthony heard, "Drop the gun, Anthony!"

The voice was loud and clear, but where had it come from? Still aiming the gun at the guy behind the counter, Anthony's eyes shifted toward the door. He expected to see a cop, but there was nobody there.

"Who said that?" he shouted. Then to the old man, "There somebody else here in the store?"

"No, I swear," the old man said.

"Well, somebody's talkin' to me," Anthony said. "Somebody who knows my name."

"Leave them alone, Anthony," the voice said. "Put the gun down, let the man call the cops, and you won't get hurt. That's your best option right now. Actually, that's your *only* option."

The voice sounded closer now, a few feet away, but there was still nobody near him. What the hell? Now Anthony was scared, his gun arm shaking.

"What's goin' on, yo?" Anthony asked. "Somebody else in here? You hidin' someplace?"

"This is the last time I'll ask you." The voice was even closer now. "Put the gun down, and you can go back to jail and serve the time you deserve to serve. Don't put the gun down, and you're still going back to jail, but you may spend a couple of weeks in the hospital."

Anthony was thinking, *So this is what being crazy's like?* He was hearing voices. What the hell else could be happening? They were gonna lock him up—not in jail this time, in a mental home.

"Shut up!" Anthony screamed, maybe at himself.

The old man and Asian woman were staring at Anthony like he was crazy.

"What you lookin' at?" Anthony said to them. Then his mask suddenly came off his head, as if somebody had pulled it off—but nobody was there. Anthony, shocked and confused, said, "What the—" as he felt a pain in his face, like he'd just been sucker punched. And then he was tumbling back into the shelf, cans of food falling on his head and to the floor.

He had dropped the gun. When he tried to reach for it, it slid away from his hand, all the way toward the entrance to the store— as if somebody had kicked it. But nobody was there.

So it wasn't just voices anymore. Now things were moving on their own, and he was imagining getting hit in the face? But if he was just imagining things, how come it hurt so bad? And, damn, why was his nose bleeding?

"Hey, I gave you a chance," the voice said, "but you wanted to do it the hard way, so you're getting the hard way."

"Who—who said that?" Anthony asked, his voice trembling. Then his head jerked to the right, as if somebody had just shot his left cheek with a BB gun at close range.

"Hey, over here," the voice said. It sounded like it had come from near his stomach.

Anthony looked down, and something hit his chin. His head snapped back into the cans again.

"I mean over here," the voice said from—it sounded like an inch in front of his face. Then something hit his forehead, and he felt dazed, the whole bodega spinning.

"This was what you asked for," the voice said.

Anthony wanted to say, "I didn't ask for nothin'," but he couldn't get his lips to move.

Every time Anthony tried to get up, something hit him and he fell back down again. Then he heard sirens, getting louder and louder.

"I'd love to stick around," the voice said, "but I have another date downtown."

LEAVING the bodega, Scott Lang—from his perspective as a half-inch-tall man—saw the police cars pulling up to the curb. As the cops rushed out, Scott darted across the sidewalk, which, from his tiny perspective, was the size of a large plaza. Then he jumped off the curb, which felt like jumping from a second-story window. He landed on his feet and continued, passing between two humongous parked cars.

Scott had promised Hank Pym that he wouldn't abuse the Ant-Man technology—which meant not using it for trivial reasons, like to beat the evening rush. But once in a while, when he was in a hurry, why not?

When a cab approached, Scott leaped onto its front end and held on with his super-strong hands and feet. Hopping from car to car as Ant-Man was the fastest way to get anywhere. He clung to the roof of the cab until it started to make a right onto 125th Street, and then he leapt onto the windshield of another car—a white SUV. He stared right at the huge, angry face of the driver, who thought a bug had just landed in front of him. It was always dangerous for Scott to remain so close at another person's eye level for too long—the person might notice that he wasn't in fact a bug, but a miniature human being in a red-and-gray suit. He heard a loud squeaking noise and turned to see the tremendous blade of the windshield wiper heading right for him. Just before it could reach him, he jumped up and landed on the SUV's roof.

He rode on the SUV to 116th, and then jumped on a car headed east toward FDR Drive. There was no traffic. The car took him all the way downtown to the East Village. Then, jumping along the tops of cars, trucks, and buses, he made his way to the Starbucks on Astor and Lafayette.

Although he'd made great time, he was still running late. He couldn't resume normal size in public, so he ran into the coffee shop, dodging the oncoming shoes, sneakers, and boots like a real-life game of Frogger. There was a line for the customers' bathroom, so he darted under the door of the bathroom labeled "Employees Only."
He had a set of clothes, pre-shrunk, in a pouch attached to the Ant-Man suit. He put on his jeans, workboots, and flannel shirt, then activated the Pym expanding gas. Soon he was back to human size. A Starbucks barista—a young Asian woman—entered the bathroom and did a double-take.

"How'd you get in here?" she asked.

"Uh, the door was unlocked," Scott said.

"Customers can't use this bathroom," she said.

"Sorry, won't happen again," Scott said.

He rushed out to meet his date.

AT A TABLE up front near the windows facing Astor, Scott's date said, "My name's Anne with an e, but my friends call me Annie."

Scott had met her on Tinder—yep, super heroes were dating online, too, nowadays. How else was a busy single dad supposed make a connection in the big city? Scott had liked Anne's pics—she looked hip, in a not-trying-too-hard kind of way, with dark hair, short bangs, big, trendy glasses from Warby Parker—and they seemed to be at a similar place in life. She was recently divorced, had a twelve-year-old son—two years younger than Scott's daughter Cassie—and she had written in her profile that she was looking for "something light, yet meaningful," which pretty much summed up Scott's idea of the perfect relationship. It had been a few months since Scott's last relationship—with Regina, the manic-depressive hypnotherapist—had ended, and now he was getting back out there, trying to meet some new people.

Scott was happy that Anne had a strong resemblance to her photos, which wasn't always the case with Internet dating. Since his divorce, Scott had gone on dates with women who'd claimed to be around his age, but turned out to be older than his mother. Things took a sharp turn for the worse when Anne spent the first ten minutes of the date taking about her bad divorce and how much she hated her ex-husband, and the next ten minutes going on about the businesses she was planning to go into "someday"—jewelry design, real estate, Reiki—and of course how she wanted to write a memoir of her divorce because she had "so many crazy stories to tell." Currently, despite all of her grand plans, she didn't seem to be doing much of anything—well, except hating her ex.

Scott had barely said anything about himself. He was trying to come up with a good excuse to get away, but she was only halfway through her iced coffee. He thought it would be rude to make some excuse and leave now, but it would be so easy. He had his Ant-Man suit on under his clothes, which gave him the perfect date-going-bad escape hatch: He could activate the suit's Pym Particles and poof, practically disappear.

"Okay, biggest fears," she said.

"Excuse me?" Scott asked.

"What's your biggest fear?" she said. "Go first."

Scott didn't feel like playing this game—he just wanted to get home, hang with his daughter. But at least they weren't talking about Anne's divorce anymore.

"Hmm, that's a tough one," he said. "I guess you don't want to hear the obvious ones like death, nuclear holocausts, alien invasions."

"Are you afraid of those things?"

"No, not really."

Scott smiled, but she remained serious. Apparently, she didn't get sarcasm—strike two. He took a big sip of his coffee, hoping it would encourage her to drink hers faster, but her coffee was stuck at the same level like a clogged hourglass.

"Then what are you afraid of?" she asked.

"Okay, failing," Scott said. "I'm afraid of failing."

"Ooh, good one," she said. "Like those dreams you have when you're in high school and there's a big test and you're afraid of failing. I hate those."

"I was thinking about it more psychologically," Scott said. "Like failing as a man, failing as a father."

"Oh," she said, and then, brightening: "You wanna hear my biggest fear?"

"Go for it," Scott said.

"My biggest fear is that the next guy I marry will be exactly like my ex."

So much for not talking about her divorce anymore.

"Really?" Scott asked. "That's your *biggest* fear?"

"You mentioned psychology," she said. "Well, I believe people fall back into old patterns. Date the same people, make the same mistakes again and again. I mean, take you, for instance. What do I know about you? I know your name's Scott, you have a daughter, and you're kind of cute, but what do I *really* know? You know what I mean? You could be hiding something, some dark secret. I mean nobody tells everybody everything on the first date, right? So there could be, I don't know, like some big bombshell, a deal-breaker, that you tell me about on date five—and by that time I'm getting in deep, emotionally involved, and kicking myself for not realizing it sooner. Red flags, that's what I'm talking about. I'm afraid I won't pick up on the red flags. What about you?"

Scott was distracted. *Kind of cute? What's up with that?* He said, "I'm sorry, what was the question?"

"What's your darkest secret?" Anne asked.

Had that been her question?

"Um, wow, that's a tough one," Scott said. He had a suit under his clothes that gave him the ability to shrink to the size of an ant while gaining superhuman strength. That qualified as a pretty big secret.

"Come on," she said. "I know when a man has secrets. You definitely have a past. I can see it in your eyes."

Oh no—she wasn't a psychic, was she? After a fling with Emma Frost from the X-Men last year, he'd made a pact with himself: no more mutants, and no more out-there, new-age women. He wanted someone normal, with no drama. Good luck with that in New York, right?

"Okay, I can tell I'm making you uncomfortable," she said. "I'll phrase it a different way. What are you hiding? What's your biggest regret?"

This was easy—his past life of crime. Lately, he'd been doing a good job putting that troubled part of his past behind him, trying to redeem himself by fighting the good fight. But he still felt guilty about some of the things he had done when he was younger, and he preferred not to dredge up those memories—especially on first dates.

"Um, how about you go first on that one?" Scott asked.

"Okay," she said. "I once stole money from a homeless guy."

"You're kidding me," Scott said, trying to imagine this neurotic downtown mom stealing money from a guy on the street. For the first time in the date, he was intrigued.

"Nope," she said. "I'm serious. It happened in Amherst—you know, where UMass is? That's where I went to college. Anyway, I was drunk with my friends, and one of them dared me to take a dollar out of the guy's cup. So I did it and ran away and felt incredibly guilty. I looked for the guy the next day, but I couldn't find him. I thought I'd see him eventually—but, nope, I never saw him again. I still carry the dollar with me wherever I go, just in case I run into him."

"Wow, that's, um, really unusual," Scott said.

"How about you?"

"Nope, never mugged a homeless guy. I hope to check that one off my bucket list someday."

She didn't laugh or even smile. Sarcasm definitely wasn't her forte. Strike three.

She asked, "Have you ever stolen anything?"

There were times in life when honesty wasn't an option.

So he went with, "Hasn't everybody?"

"Not everybody," she said. "I'm sure, like, Mother Theresa never stole anything."

"I'm not so sure about that," Scott said. "When she was six years old there was probably a cookie jar with a cookie she wasn't supposed to eat inside it, and I bet she ate it."

"Cookies don't count," Anne said.

"I think stealing cookies should definitely be countable." Scott smiled. "Can I be honest with you about something?"

"I love honesty," she said.

Of course she did. Everybody loves honesty until they hear something they don't want to hear.

"I don't think this date's going very well," he said.

"You don't?" She seemed hurt.

"Come on," he said. "You don't honestly think this is working, do you?"

"Well," she said. "I'm not really sure."

"You can't connect with somebody if you're looking for red flags from the get-go. Connections just happen."

"You're right. I'm so sorry," she said. "I always do that, get too pushy. I mean not *always* and not *too*. It's not that being a *little* pushy is good, either. I don't know what I mean. I don't go out on a lot of dates—I guess that's the problem. Actually I haven't gone out on any dates at all since my divorce, so maybe that's part of the—"

"Totally understandable," Scott said. "Also, I'd suggest not talking about your divorce so much. I mean not upfront. To be honest, it's kind of a turnoff."

"I do talk about my divorce a lot, don't I?" she said. "I just said it again. I don't know why I do that. I mean, I'm totally over my divorce. I just did it again. Oh my god, I can't stop. I messed up the whole date, didn't I? It's just nervous energy. I'm on Xanax. I know that means I should be less neurotic, but normally I'm even more neurotic than this. That's what my ex used to say. Oh my god, I just did it again. Can we start over?"

"Fine," Scott said. "Let's start over."

"My name's Anne with an e but my friends call me Annie."

Scott laughed.

"See," he said. "Now *that* was natural."

Maybe she'd been right about her nervous energy getting the best of her, because now she seemed much calmer. They started to have an actual conversation. They shared stories about their kids, talked about movies and plays they'd seen lately, art exhibits they'd checked out. Scott wasn't monitoring the level of her coffee anymore—he was having a good time.

"Well, it seems like we got off to a rusty start," he said, "but can

I be honest with you about something else?"

"Oh no, not again," she said.

"I'm really starting to like you," he said.

She blushed a little and said, "That's sweet."

He reached across the table and took her hand. Wow, talk about going from zero to sixty. This date had gone from life support to one of the best dates Scott had been on since he'd split with his ex. He was already thinking about their next meeting—he would suggest that they get together again later this week. Maybe he'd take her out to his favorite tapas place in the West Village.

Then Scott noticed the ant crawling along the table near their interlocked hands. He wasn't surprised. For reasons he didn't fully understand, ants were attracted to him when he had on his Ant-Man suit, even when he wasn't shrunk down. And lately ants came over to him even when he left the suit home, locked in a safe. He wasn't sure how or why the ants wanted to be around him. Perhaps it was because he'd been exposed to so many Pym Particles—the main component in the shrinking gas that allowed him to become Ant-Man—that the gas had had a permanent effect on him. Or maybe the ants simply were able to sense an ant-friendly nature in Scott's essence. Scott was continually amazed by the intelligence of the tiny insects. He didn't get why society as a whole scorned ants, associated them with filth and infestations, and considered them an overall nuisance.

Anne noticed the ant, grimaced, and said, "Oh my god, this is so disgusting! Starbucks is a huge corporation; they should have standards." Then she took a napkin and raised her hand to squash it.

Scott grabbed her wrist before she could kill the ant and said, "Don't ever do that."

"What?" Anne sounded confused.

"Knowingly kill an ant," Scott said. "I mean, it's one thing if you step on one on the street by accident—some tragedies can't be avoided—but when you do it on purpose, it's like murder."

"You're kidding, right?" she asked.

"Do I sound like I'm kidding?"

"Let go of me, please."

Scott let go of her wrist. Well, so much for this being a great date.

Scott knew that his reaction had to seem bizarre to her, even crazy, but he couldn't help asking, "What do you have against ants?"

"Excuse me?"

"You were about to murder that ant," he said.

"Murder?"

"Kill, extinguish—however you want to put it."

"It's just an ant."

"Is that what you'd say if I went up to your dog or your cat and tried to kill it? It's just a cat? It's just a dog?"

"Please tell me this is a joke," she said.

Scott, more upset now, said, "So you were lying on your profile when you said you love animals and believe in—how did you put it? Oh right, 'kindness to others.' This is how you express kindness? I mean, stealing the dollar from the homeless guy—okay, you were a drunk college kid. But now you're an adult, a mother. What's your excuse this time?"

"If this is a joke, it's not funny," she said.

"Do I look like I'm joking?"

"Making such a big deal about some stupid ant."

"Ants are not stupid!"

Now all of Starbucks was their audience.

"They're not?"

"Ants have bigger brains, proportionally to their weight, than humans."

Scott didn't know whether this was true, but he'd said it with assurance.

"A lot of good that does them," Anne said. "Who cares about ants?"

"I'd rather read a memoir of an ant than a memoir of your divorce," Scott said.

People in the coffee bar were looking over, wondering what the fuss was about. Now there were a few more ants crawling on the table. They had sensed the tension and possible danger, and were coming to help Scott and their fellow ant.

Anne noticed the ants, too, and stood up, putting on her jacket. She said, "You have serious problems, you know that?"

"You almost murder an innocent ant, and I have problems?"

"An innocent ant? That's it—I've had it. This is officially the worst date ever."

"You got that right."

"I'm going home."

"Yeah, well, don't kill any ants there, either."

She was about to leave, but then she turned back toward Scott. "See? I was right about patterns," she said. "Thank you. Thank you so much for revealing your true self on date number one. Saved me a lot of time."

She was rushing toward the exit.

"Never hurt an ant again."

"Freak!" she shouted.

"Assassin!" he shouted back.

THREE

RIDING home on the 6 train, Scott knew he'd gone too far. Yeah, it had been wrong of Anne to try to kill that ant, but probably tens of thousands of ants were killed every day in Manhattan alone, stomped on and exterminated by pesticides. Scott couldn't save them all. Still, watching an ant die—or almost die—was always emotional for him, and sometimes he lashed out.

When he got out at Seventy-Seventh Street, he texted her:

> Sorry for blowing up like that. That was wrong of me.

A couple minutes later he sent another one:

> Really enjoyed meeting you!!

Who was he kidding? She probably thought he was a total psycho/ weirdo—there was no way he could turn this thing around. He knew he'd never hear from her again. If anything, the apologetic texts would probably make him seem even more unstable.

Well, he'd have to put this behind him—chalk it up to experience. He obviously wasn't ready to have a girlfriend again, anyway. Next time he'd try to keep his pro-ant emotions in check.

As he walked, he texted Cassie to ask whether she'd had dinner yet. Scott hadn't, so he picked up takeout Chinese—pepper steak for him and Cassie's fave, shrimp chow fun—and then continued to his building on East Seventy-Eighth Street between First and York.

Scott had moved to the Upper East Side from the East Village several months ago, before Cassie began her freshman year at Eleanor Roosevelt High School. "El-Ro" was one of the top schools for science in the city and, like Scott, Cassie was a technology geek. She loved computers, video games, and learning about the brain. Scott hadn't gone to college, so he wanted Cassie to get on a good track and stay on it. She wanted to be a neurologist, which sounded like a great idea to Scott; hopefully she'd make enough money to support him in his old age.

Another great thing about the school—it was only a couple of blocks from their apartment, and the location was convenient for Scott, as well. He was working as a cable technician for NetWorld, a computer-networking company in Midtown. It was a nice low-key job that kept him out of trouble—and out of the spotlight. Those were his main objectives these days.

Cassie's mom—Scott's ex-wife, Peggy—had moved to Portland, Oregon, to take care of her mother, who was suffering from Alzheimer's. Scott already felt tremendous guilt for missing time with Cassie while he'd been in prison, and then putting her through a divorce. He was grateful for the time he had with her now. He had to hand it to her—she was a tough kid and was doing great in school—but he wanted to provide a stable home, to devote himself to being a good father.

Scott set the table and called for Cassie to come out of her room. As always, he had to yell a few times to get her attention, but then she came out and joined him at the table. She had long blonde hair and was effortlessly pretty. Part tomboy, part geek, she wasn't really into girly things, like shopping and wearing lots of makeup. She wasn't into sports, either, which was fine with Scott. One of their favorite father-daughter activities was to take apart computers and other electronics, and then put the devices back together. She and Scott used to love playing video games together, building crazy cities on Minecraft, and assembling intricate model airplanes and spaceships. But lately, since she'd started high school, Cassie had stopped hanging out with Scott as much, and she spent a lot of her free time at home Skyping and Facetiming with her friends. Normal teenage behavior, of course, but Scott missed his little girl.

"So," Scott said, as they started eating, "how was your day?"

"Fine," she said, looking at her cell. She tapped out a text message.

"Let's go," Scott said. "Hand it over."

"Dad, come on—"

"The phone, right now."

Cassie rolled her eyes and handed Scott her cell phone. Scott had a rule at the dinner table: If you text at the table, the other person reads the text out loud.

"Thank you, and don't roll your eyes," Scott said. He read the text out loud: "I think I'm in love with Tucker McKenzie."

Cassie was blushing.

"Okay, who's Tucker McKenzie?" Scott asked.

"Just a person," Cassie said. "Can I have my phone back?"

Still holding the phone, Scott said, "A person. Okay, that narrows it down. Is he a person who goes to your school?"

"What difference does it make?"

"He doesn't go to your school?"

"Yes, he goes to my school…oh my god…can I have my phone back?"

"Is he in one of your classes?"

"No, okay? He's like a tenth-grader."

"A tenth-grader?" Scott was horrified—a tenth-grader was practically a man. "Isn't that a little old for you, Cassie?"

"It's only one year older than me, Dad."

"It's a big deal to date someone one year older than you, especially in high school."

"To *what*?" she asked.

"Date," Scott said.

"Huh?"

"*Date.*"

"I don't know what that means."

"You don't know what date means?"

"People don't date anymore, Dad."

"They don't? Then dating is just a concept I imagined? I've been hallucinating for, well, my entire life?"

"I mean *people* people. People-in-high-school-type people."

"Ah, *real* people," Scott said. "I get it now." He had a feeling she was missing his sarcasm, just like Anne had. For a moment he wondered whether maybe *he* was the problem. "So what's dating called these days for real, high-school people?"

"I don't know. Nothing."

"It's called nothing?"

"Just, like, hanging out."

"Okay, well, if you and this Tucker McKenzie start *hanging out*,

I want to meet him, okay? By the way, I don't trust that name—Tucker McKenzie. He sounds like a total player."

"It's just a name," she said, "like any other name. And we're not going to start hanging out. We're not going to start anything."

Scott stared at her.

Finally, she said, "Okay, Dad."

Scott smiled. It felt good: parenting, creating boundaries. All those self-help books he'd read on single parenting were starting to pay off.

Then Cassie said, "What about you?"

"Me?" Scott asked.

"How was your *date?*" she said, making *date* sound like something silly that only divorced dads would do.

"How did you know I was on a date?" Scott asked.

"You're wearing a nicer-than-normal shirt and shoes, not Nike Airs. You might as well be holding a sign."

Scott had to smile.

"Don't think I made a love connection," he said, remembering how Anne had called him a freak.

"Oh well," Cassie said. "She probably isn't worth it, then."

After dinner, Cassie went to her room and shut the door, and Scott heard the lock click. A sign on her door warned, "Abandon all hope, ye who enter here." Scott accepted that Cassie was a teenager now and sometimes needed her space, her alone time. He was glad that her rebellion had manifested as a quote from *The Inferno* on her bedroom door, instead of drugs or sex. But how long would it be till the full-blown rebellion started? Was Dante only the beginning?

Scott cleaned up, did the dishes, took out the garbage. The hardest part of being a single dad was having to do everything—all the parenting, all the chores—on his own. But there were pluses. Scott and Peggy used to bicker all the time about doing housework, and it was nice to have relaxing evenings at home now. He put on some jazz, flipped through a *Time Out New York*, watched some BBC detective show on Netflix. At ten o'clock he turned to the news.

There was nothing about the busted bodega robbery on the news—even on New York 1, the local twenty-four-hour-a-day news station. There was probably a report online somewhere speculating that Ant-Man had been involved in the bust—but since no one had been killed or seriously injured, it wasn't a major story.

Scott was used to the lack of attention. Unlike other super heroes who were focused on saving the world, Scott usually went after small-time criminals, taking down repeat offenders before they could rob, rape, or kill again. His goal was to clean up crime from the ground up—take out one criminal at a time, make the streets safer, and improve the quality of life for the average citizen. Helping the little man didn't get Scott the splashy headlines, but it brought him a lot of satisfaction.

Scott switched to CNN, where Tony Stark was holding a press conference, fielding questions from the media about the latest Hydra plot he'd busted. Tony was in great form—cocky, arrogant, dismissive, but still somehow captivating. Scott had known Tony for years, and Tony had helped him get out of a few jams. Who couldn't use some help from Iron Man once in a while? But while Scott couldn't fly into outer space and fight off tanks, he could do things that Tony and other super heroes couldn't. Once, he had even saved Tony's life during a mission with Cap in Afghanistan—Tony had been trapped in his suit when Scott shrunk down and rescued him.

Tony seemed to have amnesia about that day—he clearly didn't want to acknowledge that Scott had saved his ass—but that was okay with Scott. Scott loved what he did, but he didn't thrive on the star power, didn't get off on having his name on buildings and in the headlines. Tony, like Cap and Spidey, commanded attention, but Scott actually preferred to lurk unnoticed in the background, and he certainly didn't need the spotlight. His main goal was to be a great dad, a great man. If they were in a rock band, Tony would be the lead singer, Spidey would be on lead guitar, Cap would be the drummer, and Scott would be the bass player. Or not even the bass player. He'd be the guy with the cowbell.

"You ever consider giving it all up?" a reporter asked Tony.

"I'd quit tomorrow if I could," Tony said. "But if I don't catch all the bad guys, who will?"

Scott laughed, said, "You tell 'em, Tone, you tell 'em," then flicked off the TV.

Scott knocked on Cassie's door and said, "Bedtime in ten minutes," and then pulled out the Murphy bed. The apartment was small, even by New York standards, but it was all he could afford. Besides, Scott was kind of used to living small.

Later, Scott lay in bed, reading a self-help book—*100 Reasons Why Your Teenage Daughter Hates Your Guts*. He dozed off, the book open on his chest—only to wake up, startled, when somebody rang the buzzer.

He glanced at the time on his cell phone—12:14. He'd been asleep for about an hour—who could be buzzing at this time of night? It was probably some drunk kids, or maybe someone was making a mistake.

The buzzer sounded again, longer this time, so Scott went to the intercom and said, "Yeah?"

"Scott Lang?"

It was a man. He sounded serious, official. Scott's name wasn't on the buzzer, so he knew this wasn't a prank caller.

"Maybe," Scott said. "What do you want?"

"FBI," the man said. "We need to speak with you right away."

FOUR

THERE had been a time in Scott's life when, if FBI agents had shown up at his apartment late at night, he would have panicked—maybe even made a beeline for the fire escape or roof. Even now, the situation churned up some fight-or-flight instinct. But the panic subsided when he reminded himself that he'd done nothing wrong, hadn't broken any laws—well, lately, anyway—and he had nothing to fear.

"Be down in a sec," Scott said into the intercom.

He put on jeans, a T-shirt, and flip-flops, and went downstairs. He could have buzzed the guy up, but he didn't know whether the guy was actually with the FBI. Cassie's safety always came first.

Two men were waiting in the vestibule. One—tall, wide shouldered, close-cropped hair, wearing a dark suit—had a look that screamed FBI agent. The other guy—wiry, balding, glasses—looked more like an accountant.

When Scott opened the inner door, the guy in the suit showed an FBI badge. Scott knew what a real badge looked like—and, yep, this one was real.

The guy said, "I'm Agent Warren, and this is Agent James. Can we come up please? It's important."

Scott was already weary of the whole situation: FBI agents with something important to discuss? Nothing good could come of this.

"It's the middle of the night. My daughter's asleep."

"Sorry, but we'd rather discuss it upstairs, if you don't mind."

Well, at least they hadn't read him his rights. Still, they hadn't come by to hang out. Did it have something to do with the bodega robbery—or his identity as Ant-Man? He hoped this was a dream and he was still in bed, asleep, the book on his chest.

He let the agents into the apartment. The place was so small that it was hard to get to the couch with the Murphy bed open, so he sat with the agents at the table in the nook he called the dining room. There were only two chairs, so Scott had to sit on a stool.

"Well, I love surprises," Scott said, "but this is taking it a bit too far, don't you think?"

The agents remained stoic.

"You and your family may be in serious danger," Warren said.

Scott hadn't expected that. He didn't know what he'd been expecting, but it wasn't that.

"Okay," Scott said. "How so?"

"Willie Dugan escaped from prison seven months ago."

This wasn't news to Scott. Dugan was an old, well, associate of Scott's. They'd pulled off several heists together and then parted ways. Scott had been forced to testify against Dugan at the trial nine years ago.

"I heard about that," Scott said. "So?"

"You were friends with Dugan, weren't you?" James asked.

"I wouldn't say we were ever friends," Scott said. "Acquaintances, yes. If you think I have any idea where he's hiding, I don't. In fact, I was already questioned about that, several times."

"There have been some recent developments," Warren said.

"You found him?" Scott asked.

"No, unfortunately, we haven't," James said.

"I don't get it," Scott said. "What does this have to do with me and my family being in danger?"

"What about Nicky Soto?" James asked.

Nicky had also been in the crew with Dugan.

"Yeah, I know him," Scott said. "Well, *knew* him."

"And Miguel Santana?" James asked.

"Yeah," Scott said.

"Robert Billings?" Warren asked.

"No, don't remember him," Scott said.

"Went by the nickname 'Dollar,'" Warren said.

Oh, *him*. Scott had heard stories about Dollar Billings, but he'd never known the man personally.

"Can you please tell me what's going on here?" Scott asked.

"Soto, Santana, and Billings have all been killed—murdered—within the last several months," Warren said. "And we think you may be next on Dugan's hit list."

"Whoa, hold up," Scott said. "Murdered? Murdered by who?"

"Dugan, we believe," Warren said. "Or Dugan's associates."

"You *believe?*" Scott asked.

"It's most likely related to Dugan," James said. "He's our prime suspect. We have a witness account to one of the murders, and evidence in the other murders that suggests Dugan was involved."

"Not to mention the fact that all three victims had been affiliated with Dugan in some capacity," Warren said.

"Two of them testified against him," James said. "The third,

Billings—Dugan had a personal grudge against him. Had to do with a woman."

"Wow. I can't believe Nicky and Miguel are dead," Scott said. "I mean, I hadn't seen them in years, and I know they made mistakes, but they were trying to turn their lives around." Scott let that sink in for several seconds, then said, "But I see where you're going with this. Let me guess. You think I'm next on Dugan's hit list because I testified against him, am I right?"

Warren and James didn't say anything.

"Well, I'm not," Scott said.

"Why do you say that?" James asked.

"Because I know Willie, and I know he wouldn't do that."

"I thought you said you didn't know Dugan," Warren said.

"I haven't talked to him in years," Scott said, "but I know him. I know how he thinks."

"Well, we have information that tells us that you're wrong—he's coming after you next."

Scott wondered whether this could be correct. He *thought* he knew Dugan—but it was true he hadn't spoken to the man in about ten years, since their last job together. It was possible, even likely, that Dugan had changed. After all, he'd done all that time in prison, and time in prison changed everybody—usually for the worse.

"What kind of information?" Scott asked.

"That doesn't matter," Warren said.

"It matters to me," Scott said.

"We debriefed a witness who was privy to information regarding Dugan's plans. Your name came up," James said.

"In what context?" Scott asked.

"I'm sorry, but that's all we can share with you right now," Warren said. "It's for your safety. We'll tell you what you need to know, and that's it."

"What about my daughter and ex-wife?" Scott asked. "Why do you think they could be in danger, too?"

"Before Santana was murdered, his family received anonymous threats," James said.

"And those threats could've been made by Dugan or persons associated with him," Warren added.

"Whoa, hold up a second," Scott said. "Dugan escaped from prison almost a year ago, right? Then while he's out, three murders take place—murders of guys who'd testified against him or wronged him in some way. And it took you all this time to connect the dots?"

"The victims lived in different part of the country," Warren said. "California, Texas, Florida."

"There are databases these days," Scott said. "It's called technology."

The agents, especially Warren, didn't seem to enjoy listening to Scott, some ex-con, patronizing them.

"Look, we're not here to explain ourselves to you," Warren said. "We're here to protect you and your family."

"Thanks," Scott said, "but I can protect my family on my own."

Times like this Scott wished he could scream out, *I'm Ant-Man, morons! I don't need any protection!* He'd kept his identity as Ant-Man a secret, mainly to protect Cassie. As a super hero, he had a long list of enemies who might be out for revenge—and again, while he wasn't concerned about his own safety, keeping Cassie out of danger was his priority. Ironically, Cassie was one the few people who knew about his secret. He trusted her with it.

"I'm afraid you have no choice," Warren said.

"No choice?" Scott asked. "What are you going to do, force me?"

"Actually, yes," Warren said.

"We've received an order of protection for your family until the threat subsides," James said.

Scott laughed, even though he knew this definitely wasn't a joke. "You've gotta be kidding me, right?" He thought, *An order of protection for a super hero?* Tony Stark and the gang were going to tease him about this for years. He wanted to keep Cassie safe, of course, but what if the threat wasn't real? An Order of Protection would cause a major disruption in her life, and he didn't want to put her through that unless it was absolutely necessary.

"How do you know Dugan's in New York?" he asked. "And if you do know he's in New York, why can't you just catch him?"

"The protection order is effective immediately," Warren said, standing.

Scott stood up, as well. "This is about covering your own asses, isn't it? You guys messed up, didn't connect the dots fast enough, and a few guys from Dugan's past got whacked. Now, with extremely circumstantial evidence, you're going to make me and my family accept bodyguards?"

Warren said, "The marshals who'll be protecting you are outside right now. Carlos Torres will escort you to work, and Roger Shelly will take your daughter to school. Tomorrow evening the agents will be relieved by other agents for night duty."

"Look, seriously," Scott said, "this a waste of taxpayers' money."

"Your ex-wife Peggy Lang is currently being placed under protective custody, as well," James said.

"Whoa, my ex-wife doesn't even live in New York. She lives in—"

"Oregon," James said.

"See, maybe we do know how to use those databases," Warren said, leaking sarcasm.

"There's no reason to involve her," Scott said.

"She's already involved," Warren said. "Agents are at her residence right now."

"Come on, this is insane," Scott said. "I appreciate you guys coming here and giving me a heads-up and all, but I'm fine, and my family will be fine. We don't need any protection."

"I don't think you get it," Warren said. "You have no choice in the matter."

"Actually, you're getting off easy," James said. "The alternative was you, your daughter, and your ex-wife going into the Witness Protection Program."

"Look at it like we're doing you a favor." Warren smirked.

"I'm telling you, you guys are getting it wrong," Scott said. "Willie Dugan won't hurt me."

But it was too late; the agents had already left the apartment.

Scott cursed. He banged his fist against the wall so hard that Cassie came out of her room.

Squinting, she asked, "What's going on?"

"Nothing," Scott said. "Go back to sleep."

"Did I just hear like voices out here?"

"No," Scott said, "you must've been dreaming."

Cassie didn't seem convinced, but she muttered, "G'night," and went back into her bedroom.

Scott went right to his iPad and googled Willie Dugan. He read pretty much what the agents had told him, about the murder of Robert Billings in Florida, two days ago, in which Dugan was the prime suspect. It figured the Feds were on the case now, with the murders taking place in different states. Maybe jurisdictional issues had prevented law enforcement from connecting the dots sooner.

Scott understood why the Feds thought Dugan would try to kill him. Dugan had already killed three people—two who'd testified against him. If this were true, Scott didn't understand why Dugan had waited so long. Why wasn't Scott first on his list?

Scott and Willie had been, if not friends, then good acquaintances, until Dr. Henry Pym had given Scott the Ant-Man suit—under the condition that he use the technology for good, not evil. Scott had decided to leave his criminal life behind, but he hadn't been sure how to break the news to Dugan.

Scott, Dugan, and a couple of other guys were at a motel in Kentucky, about an hour outside Louisville. They were on a "business trip'" doing recon for a bank robbery, when a fire broke out at the motel. Scott and the other guys got out, but Willie was trapped inside.

Firefighters arrived and tried to chop their way in, but the smoke was so bad they had to bail. Dugan was terrified, screaming for his life. So Scott rushed to his car and opened the trunk where he was keeping the Ant-Man suit. Up until then he'd only worn the suit a few times—he wasn't exactly an expert with navigating around in it. But if he wanted to save Dugan's life, he didn't have any time to lose. So he shrunk down, climbed up the rim of the fire ladder and past the firefighters who had given up on battling the blaze, and entered Willie's room on the second floor of the hotel.

Willie was losing consciousness, too out of it to see Scott return to normal size. Scott busted the window in the bathroom, dragged Willie out to safety, and dropped him down to the firefighters below. Then Scott shrunk and slipped away. The fire spread, and the entire motel burnt down.

A couple of days later, Scott announced to Willie that he was leaving the crew. Willie was adamantly opposed to the idea. Scott's technical abilities had helped them bypass alarm systems and crack safes, and he was worried that Scott would flip and testify against him. Scott promised Dugan that he would never rat him out to the cops—a promise that, ultimately, Scott couldn't keep.

Over the next few years, Scott fell out of touch with Dugan. Scott turned his attention to raising his daughter and fighting crime. He was redeeming himself, becoming a better man, and he hoped that Dugan had made similar changes in his life. Then he heard on the news that Dugan had been arrested for committing a double homicide in Yonkers, New York. After an argument over a woman, Dugan had shot two men—executionstyle—in the parking lot outside an apartment building. Scott had known Dugan as a criminal genius who'd pulled off dozens of heists.

But the Dugan he knew wasn't violent, had never killed anyone, and Scott had never even seen him argue or get into a fight. Dugan had always seemed laid back, quiet. Had something happened to change him into a cold-blooded killer, or had he simply hidden this side of himself from Scott?

Scott had been called to testify at the trial. The evidence against Dugan was overwhelming—witness accounts, DNA samples, security-video footage of one of the murders—and Scott wanted to do whatever he could to help put Dugan behind bars. He felt a personal responsibility to help send Dugan away for life, so he couldn't kill again. Scott had a lot of guilt: If he hadn't saved Dugan in that fire, the people Dugan had killed would still be alive.

Logically, Scott knew he wasn't responsible, but that didn't change the way he felt.

During the trial, Dugan didn't make eye contact with Scott. Not during the testimony, or when he was entering or exiting the court-room—never. Scott knew this was purposeful, that Dugan was try-ing to send him a message—but what was the message?

Dugan was convicted on two counts of first-degree murder. The judge handed down a series of compounding sentences that added up to life in prison. But Scott still had a gnawing feeling that he hadn't heard the last of Willie Dugan.

So it didn't really surprise Scott when he learned, last year, that Dugan and several inmates had spent nine years diligently building a tunnel and had escaped from Attica, one of the most notorious and highest-security prisons in the country. If anybody had the patience and determination to pull off such a complicated and well-coordi-nated escape, it was Willie Dugan. Dugan was a mastermind, a ge-nius, and one of the most determined people Scott had ever met. He wasn't an off-the-cuff kind of guy—he was a planner. So it also didn't surprise Scott that the other guys who'd escaped with him had been caught within twenty-four hours, while Dugan remained a fugitive. Dugan always had a plan, and he was usually a couple of steps ahead of the cops. He was a patient man, perhaps the most patient man Scott had ever met. He wasn't a risk taker. He didn't gamble unless he was one-hundred-percent certain that the odds were in his favor.

Scott knew that Dugan loved to play the long game—he probably had some big plan in mind. Did that plan include killing Scott and his family as the grand finale to his murder spree? That was the big question.

There was no way Scott could sleep now—he had way too much on his mind. He paced the apartment, snacked on a small pizza left in the fridge from a few days ago. One thing he wasn't great at was keeping up with the food shopping. He munched on the pizza until he realized how sucky it tasted, and then threw the rest in the trash.

He went down to check out the situation. It wasn't hard to spot the Feds—had to be that black Charger across the street with the tinted windows. He was officially under protective custody. This was actually happening.

Back in the apartment, his cell phone chimed, announcing an incoming text. It was from his ex:

WHAT THE HELL IS GOING ON!!!!!!

She was pissed off—no surprise there. Was there any ex-wife in the world who wouldn't flip out over having to go into protective custody because of her ex-husband?

Trying to calm her down, Scott responded:

I'll make this go away, don't worry I promise.

She fired back:

You better, or ELSE!!!!

He didn't appreciate the threat. What did "or else" mean? Would she get vindictive and reveal to the Feds that Scott was Ant-Man? Peggy loved Cassie, and Scott didn't think she'd do anything that potentially could endanger her daughter. That said, Scott's criminal past had been a major issue in his relationship with Peggy, and he'd worked hard to convince her he'd gone straight for good. The last thing he needed now was for her to have new information she could use against him. In a worst-case scenario, she could argue that he was an unfit parent and that she should have full custody of Cassie. Scott had been trying hard to provide stability for Cassie, and the last thing he wanted to do was put her in the middle of another custody battle. And if Peggy was determined to take Cassie to Oregon, a judge could easily rule in her favor since a) the courts often ruled in favor of the mothers in custody cases, and b) Scott was an ex-con with a long rap sheet.

The arrival of the Feds hadn't brought on a full-fledged fight-or-flight reaction from Scott, but *this* did. Cassie wasn't just Scott's daughter. She was his best friend—and the main reason he'd decided to turn his life around. The thought of losing her was unimaginable. He knew she was better off with him in New York.

Scott wrote back:

Trust me Just relax All will be well

and left it at that.

He knew from experience that antagonizing Peggy was always a mistake. It was a better strategy to back off and keep the peace.

She didn't text back, so maybe she'd let things settle down.

Maybe the police would catch Dugan, and this whole thing would blow over. The protection order would be lifted, and they'd all be able to go on with their lives.

Scott lay in bed, but he couldn't sleep. He had a gnawing feeling that before things got better, they were going to get much, much worse.

FIVE

USUALLY when Cassie Lang's alarm went off, she groaned, hit snooze, and stayed in bed for as long as possible. But today she couldn't wait to get to school and see Tucker McKenzie. She would probably see him during lunch and before humanities because there was some kind of tenth-grade class on the same floor. She'd only spoken to him twice so far: once when they passed each other near their lockers and he said "Hey" to her and she said "Hey" back, and another time when she saw him after school outside a pizza place on York Avenue and he said, "Yo, what's up?" and she was so excited he'd noticed her that she'd stuttered, "Oh, uh-uh, hi." But she knew it was only a matter of time until they started hanging out.

She got dressed in her favorite jeans and that cool new top from Uniqlo, but the top didn't look as good as when she'd tried it on in the store, so she put on the purple one from H&M. She didn't really like it either, but she didn't have anything else to wear. This was how it had been since her mom had moved to Portland, Oregon, and she found herself living full time with her dad. Last time she went shopping, he gave her two hundred dollars, which was like nothing in Manhattan. She understood that they were living on a budget, and that it was hard to pay for things as a single parent, but it still sucked when she couldn't find anything nice to wear. Her dad had a lot of great qualities, but he didn't get how important it was for her to look cool at school.

In the bathroom, she checked herself in the full-length and decided that she didn't look so bad. Kind of cute, actually—especially after she put on her makeup, including the new shadow she'd bought yesterday. She hoped the makeup made her look older, too, like a tenth-grader. She was pretty sure it did.

She went to the fridge to get some breakfast, a quick bowl of Honey Nut Cheerios, when she heard: "Cassie."

She turned around, startled. Her dad stood there with some gray-haired guy she'd never seen before. The guy didn't look very old—he just had gray hair.

"What are you doing home?" Cassie asked. Her dad usually left for work before she woke up.

"We need to have a little talk," Scott said.

Cassie thought, *Did I do something wrong?* Her dad had been getting weirdly strict with her lately about stuff like texting at the dinner table, but was there really anything to *talk* about? And what did that have to do with the gray-haired stranger? Was this some kind of punishment?

"What did I do?" Cassie asked.

"You didn't do anything," Scott said. "But something happened. Nothing bad, but, well…Roger's going to take you to school."

"Roger?" Cassie asked.

"I'm Roger," the man said.

"Yeah, I kinda figured that," Cassie said. Then to her dad: "But why is he *taking* me to school? What's going on? Is this like some kind of joke?"

Her dad took a deep breath, then said, "There's a situation, Cassie."

Cassie barely listened as her dad went on about how this was just temporary, but there was a chance some guy might have a grudge against him, and this was just a precaution, and it would be over soon. All she was really thinking about was how embarrassing it would be to go to school with this weird guy along with her.

She interrupted whatever her dad was saying with, "I'm going to school alone today."

"I'm sorry," her dad said. "You have to do it. We both do. I'm not exactly crazy about the situation myself, but apparently we have no choice."

"I don't need any protection," Cassie said.

"It's for your own good," the guy, Roger, said.

"This is all your fault," Cassie said to her dad. "It's all because of the past, isn't it? Because of all the criminals you used to hang out with?"

"Yes, it is sort of related to that," her dad said. "Okay, totally related to that."

"See?" Cassie couldn't control herself. "This is why Mom left. Because you're always screwing things up. And you think just because you're—"

Cassie was about to say, "You're Ant-Man," but before she could, her dad cut her off:

"Okay, I think that's enough. Eat your breakfast and then go to school with Roger, and we'll discuss this later. Is that understood?"

"No," Cassie said. "It's not understood."

But she knew there was no point in arguing about it anymore— once her dad got all serious, that was it, the discussion was over—so she went back to her cereal. She had no appetite, though. After a couple of bites, she marched into the living room, grabbed her knapsack, and left the apartment without looking at her dad or Roger.

Roger followed her downstairs and out of the building, hurrying to catch up to her.

"My school's only three blocks away. This is so stupid," she said.

Roger was telling her how he understood, and his goal was to inconvenience her as little as possible. Cassie stopped listening and started looking around for people. Meaning people who went to her high school. Oh my god, there was Ryan across the street, walking with Nikki and Carly, and ahead of them there were Charles and Justin.

"This is so embarrassing," Cassie said.

"I have a daughter, too, so I get it," Roger said. "My daughter's twenty-three now."

"Did a strange guy your daughter had never met ever walk her to school in the ninth grade?"

"Well, no," he said.

"Then how do you get it?" Cassie said.

He tried to explain, but Cassie wasn't listening. She walked with her head down, hoping no one saw her.

When they were around the corner from school, she said, "Okay, I can walk alone from here."

"Sorry, have to stay with you all day," Roger said.

Cassie stopped walking and said, "Wait, all day? I thought you were just walking me to school. You can't go into the school with me—they won't let you."

"The school already knows about the situation," he said. "Don't worry, I'll be discreet."

"Discreet? You're gonna follow me around school all day, and you expect to be discreet?"

"I do this all the time," he said. "Well, not all the time, but a lot of the time, and I know how to stay out of the way, okay?"

"I'm going home," Cassie said, and headed back toward her apartment.

Walking next to her, Roger said, "Look, come on, trust me. You're imagining this is going to be much worse than it will actually be."

Cassie shot him a look.

"I didn't mean it like that," Roger said. "I just mean it won't be so bad. And if you skip school, you'll miss out on learning and just hurt yourself."

Cassie remembered that she had a big precalculus test today she couldn't miss—and, besides, she was dying to see Tucker. "Whatever," she said, and turned back toward school.

She hoped Roger was right, and today wouldn't be as bad as she imagined. When she entered the building on Seventy-Sixth Street, she pretended that it was a normal day, and Roger wasn't right there behind her. She stared straight ahead, trying not to notice the weird looks she knew everyone was giving her.

At least Roger didn't come into homeroom with her.

But Cassie's friend Zoe noticed, because she asked, "Who's that guy?"

"What guy?" Cassie asked, trying to play dumb. Then said, "Oh, *him*. He's just a, like, school supervisor, or something."

That didn't make any sense, but she couldn't think of any other explanation.

"A school what?" Zoe asked.

"He just like monitors students sometimes and...it's nothing, never mind."

Zoe didn't push it, but eventually everyone in school would be asking her about Roger—especially if this went on for days, weeks, or even months. What if this guy had to follow her around for the rest of high school? Maybe she could make up a story—tell people he was, like, Secret Service. She could say her dad was running for governor of New York, and that was why she needed protection. But would anybody believe that? They could just google "governor candidates New York" and find out it was a total lie.

Ugh, she hated Google—she hated everything. And any way she looked at it, she was screwed.

Roger followed Cassie to her first class, drama, but it wasn't so bad. The hallways were crowded, and Roger wasn't right next to her, so people didn't seem to notice.

Then Cassie saw that Tucker and a few of his friends—including Nikki and Carly—were looking at her and laughing. She hoped she was just being self-conscious. Maybe they weren't really laughing at her. Maybe they were laughing about something else.

But then later, before chemistry, it happened again. Tucker and a couple of his friends—*different* friends—kind of smirked at her and walked away.

Cassie—with Roger trailing her like an annoying shadow—found Zoe near the lockers and said, "Why are people giving me weird looks? Did you tell them something about you-know-what?"

"No," Zoe said. "I don't even know what to tell them. You didn't tell me anything."

Cassie felt bad for accusing her.

"Sorry," she said. "It's just really weird. Tucker McKenzie and all these other people keep looking at me funny like they know something, but I don't know what it could possibly be."

"Oh my god," Zoe said. "I think I know what it is."

"What?" Cassie asked.

"You sure you want to know?"

"Yes, tell me."

Zoe took out her phone, opened Instagram, and showed Cassie the display. It was a post by Nikki with a screenshot of Cassie's text from last night:

Cassie Lang: I think I'm in luv w Tucker McKenzie

"Oh my god," Cassie said. "I can't believe Nikki did that to me. It's so humiliating."

"When I read it, I thought you and Tucker were like a couple," Zoe said.

"We're not a couple," Cassie said. "I texted her last night, in like total confidence. Why did she do that to me?"

"'Cause she's jealous and wants Tucker for herself," Zoe said. "Just a wild guess."

The bell sounded for the next period.

As Cassie headed to class, Roger came up next to her and asked, "Something wrong?"

"None of your business," Cassie said.

"I saw you looking at that girl's phone," Roger said. "You didn't get an email or some message from an address you don't recognize, did you? If you did, I have to know about it."

"It's just an Instagram post, okay?" Cassie said. "It has nothing to do with you or my dad. I have a life, too, you know!"

Cassie marched ahead and went into the classroom.

At lunch, Cassie and Zoe went to Beanocchio's, their usual coffee-lunch place on York, knowing that Nikki would be there, too. Nikki was at the table in back with a few other girls, and they all smiled and giggled when they saw Cassie approaching.

"Why did you do it?" Cassie asked.

"Do what?" Nikki pretended to be clueless.

The other girls were listening in.

"Come on, it was just a joke," Nikki said. "Why're you taking it so seriously?"

"Take it down," Cassie said.

"Take what down?"

"You know what."

"Oh *that*," Nikki continued. "You texted it to me. I thought it was, like, public knowledge."

"I can't believe you did that to me."

"It's not a big deal."

"Please take it down."

"It's my Instagram—I'll do whatever I want."

Cassie didn't understand why Nikki was acting so mean. She'd thought they were good friends. Was Nikki showing off for the other girls, trying to act cool?

"I'll tell the dean at school," Cassie said. "It's cyberbullying."

The girls laughed.

"Oh, please! I was just being funny," Nikki said. "You want me to take it down? Fine." She took out her phone, tapped the screen a few times, then said, "Okay, it's deleted, but the damage is done. Tucker's never going to like you now."

"You're horrible," Cassie said.

"Tucker McKenzie doesn't think so," Nikki said. "And why is that guy following you around, anyway? It's, like, creepy."

Cassie hadn't been in a fight since she was about eight years old and a girl at a playground had tried to push her off a slide, but she wanted to attack Nikki right now. Not in a girly way with face-slapping and hair-pulling: Cassie wanted to tackle her, punch her in the face. She couldn't do it, of course, because she'd get suspended and, oh yeah, there was an FBI agent a few feet away watching her.

So she left the coffee shop and skipped eating lunch. She walked back toward the school, with Roger following her the whole time.

She zoned out a lot the rest of the school day, trying to forget how miserable she was. Teachers called on her to participate in class a couple of times, and she was lost—had no idea what was going on—and everyone laughed. She couldn't wait for this day to be over.

Finally the day ended, and she rushed home. Roger had to check the apartment to make sure that guy who was after her father wasn't hiding in there—as if the guy was like Houdini or some-thing, and could get in and out of a locked apartments without anyone noticing.

Roger went back outside and Cassie had the whole apartment to herself. It felt great to be alone, really alone. Today had definitely been the worst day of school, and she didn't even want to think about what tomorrow would be like. Thanks to Nikki, Cassie had made a fool of herself with Tucker McKenzie.

Cassie wanted to drop out of school. It was embarrassing enough to have an FBI agent following her around, but she couldn't face Tucker again. Couldn't see him snickering at her.

She realized she'd barely eaten all day—just a few bites of cereal this morning. There was no food in the apartment—as usual—and her dad wasn't home yet. He was probably on another one of his Tinder dates. It was so unfair that her life had gotten so screwed up, but her dad could go on dates and live a normal life when he was the one who'd caused this whole mess. Not just the FBI crap, but *everything.* His crazy past, and the divorce—and what about Ant-Man? It wasn't like everybody's dad could shrink to the size of an ant and fight crime. Cassie and her mom had been keeping his secret for a year, and it didn't seem fair. *She* was the teenager. *She* was the one who was supposed to have the secrets.

Then Cassie had a great idea. It was so totally amazing and perfect, she didn't know how she hadn't thought of it sooner.

Cassie went to the closet in the hallway and moved out a couple of boxes of books or whatever, and there was the safe where her dad kept his Ant-Man suit. Once, a few years ago, Cassie had seen her dad open the safe. She remembered the combination, or most of it—34 right, 28 or maybe 27 left, 11 right. She tried it now, with 27—but, nope, it didn't open. She tried again with 28 and nothing happened. Had her dad changed the combination? That would suck big time.

After trying 27 and 28 again, she was about to give up and put the boxes back, but then she tried with 24 as the first number and 27 as the second number. She didn't know why she tried this—it was kind of unconscious—but when she turned the dial back to the right to 11, she heard a click and opened the safe.

There it was—the red-and-gray Ant-Man suit and a silver helmet-like thing with what looked like short antennae. Scott had shown Cassie the suit before, but never told her how to operate it, how to shrink to the size of an ant. He'd also told her that he could communicate with ants while he was wearing it, which had sounded crazy to her, even impossible. Had her father been lying to her?

She examined it closely. It was made of some tough material, like a weird cross between metal and fabric—definitely not something you would wear on Halloween. The helmet was strong but super thin, and had a mechanism that let it retract and practically disappear into the collar of the suit. Cassie figured this was so her dad could wear the suit under his clothes. The underside of the helmet looked like the inside of a computer. Cassie and her dad had taken apart lots of computers and put them back together—it was kind of a hobby of theirs—and the helmet was obviously the motherboard. Cassie tried on the helmet, but it was a little big. Her dad was a few inches taller than her, and when she held up the suit, it was obvious that it wouldn't fit her.

She didn't understand where the power came from—the helmet had no battery pack or power source, but it had to get its juice from somewhere. She had no idea how to turn it on, either, because there was no switch. There were a few small canister-type things, though— these contained the gas with the Pym Particles. Her dad had never told her how it worked—he always said it would be "too dangerous" to tell her, whatever that meant—but she knew the gas made things shrink. One thing Cassie was certain of, though: The suit was no hoax. It had seriously complex technology, which meant everything her dad had told her about Ant-Man could actually be true.

Cassie heard footsteps outside the front door—someone in the hallway approaching. She put the suit back in the safe as fast as she could. It could be one of the FBI agents pacing back and forth, or maybe a neighbor. Then Cassie heard a key turning in the lock. Crouching, she pushed the boxes back into the closet, blocking the safe, and was just standing up when her father entered.

"Hey," Cassie said, trying to act natural.

Her father must've seen her crouching—he seemed a little suspicious. "Hey, what's going on?"

"Not much," Cassie said. "Just, um, looking for my gloves."

"Gloves? It was seventy degrees today."

Cassie wished she'd come up with a better excuse. Gloves in May was pretty dumb.

"It's for a project for school," Cassie said.

"A project?"

"We're working with ice, in a freezer, in science class, so we need to bring in gloves."

This didn't make much more sense, but clearly it was good enough for her father, because he said, "Ah, okay. How did your day go?"

"Not so awful," Cassie said.

"Great," Scott said. "I was worried. Sorry again for getting you involved in all of this."

"No worries." Cassie kissed her dad on the cheek. Then she went into her room and shut the door.

It was hard to believe that just a few minutes ago, she had been so doom-and-gloom about the future. Now that she had this great plan about how to get revenge on Nikki, she couldn't wait to go back to school tomorrow.

SIX

I'm looking for a recommendation for a babysitter, maybe you can help me out, Little Guy? I hear you're using a good one.

The text was from Tony Stark.

Scott was at work, in the cable warehouse at the Midtown office of NetWorld, with Carlos Torres, the federal marshal who was supposedly protecting him. Obviously Tony had heard about the protection order via whatever sources he had, and naturally he was getting a big kick out of it.

Scott texted back:

Haha

Then added:

If this whole Iron Man thing doesn't work out for you, maybe you should do some stand-up

Tony responded:

> If you keep giving me such great material I might just
> do that

Scott had to smile. Tony had been teasing Scott for years about his, well, smaller stature in the super-hero world, and while Scott wasn't happy about it, he was used to it. How could he get upset with Tony after the guy had helped him out so many times? Tony had even given him a job at Stark Industries back when Scott had decided to go straight and no one else would hire an ex-con who had done a long stretch for armed robbery. Okay, yeah, so Tony had been doing a favor for Hank Pym because they were old buddies. But in a way Tony had saved Scott's life, given him the foundation he needed to get on a positive track and be a good father to Cassie. They were more than fellow Avengers—they were friends.

But the main reason Scott couldn't get upset about Tony's teasing was that he agreed with him—he *did* feel like the FBI was babysitting him, escorting him around the city. After all, as Ant-Man, he could hold his own against pretty much anybody. He agreed that Cassie needed protection—better safe than sorry—but the idea that Willie Dugan posed a serious threat to him was ridiculous. Scott tried to remind himself that he was in this situation partly because the FBI didn't know he was Ant-Man. This wasn't just about his safety—it was about his family's, as well, so he had to suck it up and deal with the ribbing from Tony. But that didn't change the way it made him feel.

The idea had occurred to Scott, though, that he didn't just have to hang around with his family in protective custody and wait for Dugan to show up. Another option was to go on the offensive—put on the

Ant-Man suit in the middle of the night, slip away, and track down Dugan. He could confront Dugan—wherever he was hiding out—and intimidate him, convince him to stay away from Scott and his family.

There were problems with this idea, though. First and foremost, he'd have to find Dugan. The FBI had been conducting a nationwide manhunt for the guy and hadn't been able to locate him, so how was Scott supposed to do it on his own? For all Scott knew, Dugan was nowhere near New York. Scott could ask Tony, Spidey, or even Cap for help, but an ex-con who'd escaped prison wasn't exactly a reason to get the big guns involved. It wasn't like the whole world was in danger—just Scott's family, apparently. Scott hoped the situation would resolve itself soon—without an appearance by Ant-Man.

He was getting ready to head out with his crew for a networking installation downtown when his boss—Jeff, the CEO of the company—called him into his office.

There was a strict divide at the company between the white-collar sales-and-marketing guys and the blue-collar cable-installation guys. Scott hadn't had a single conversation with Jeff since he'd been hired at the company about two years ago—well, except for saying "Hey" to each other on the elevator and in the men's room.

Jeff's office had glass walls and faced the rows of cubicles. Jeff closed the door. He did not ask Scott to sit. Scott would've thought he was about to get fired, except he knew that Juan in Human Resources, nicknamed "The Assassin," handled all the firings.

"Look," Jeff said, gesturing toward Carlos, who was waiting behind the glass. "I know that guy's FBI, and I'm not supposed to ask what's going on, and I won't. I don't need to know what I don't need know, if you get what I'm saying."

Scott wasn't sure what Jeff was talking about. "I *hear* what you're saying."

"What I mean," Jeff went on, "is I'm not looking for any trouble here, you know?"

"There won't be any trouble," Scott said.

"That's good," Jeff said. "'Cause I knew about your past when I took you on here, but you promised me your past would stay in your past."

"That's true—I did promise you that," Scott said.

"Well, it doesn't look like you're keeping your promise," Jeff said.

"This isn't what you think it is," Scott said. "They're just being extra cautious about a situation that really has nothing to do with me. I'm sure in a day or two this will all blow over."

Scott tried his best to say this with confidence and conviction, but he knew he wasn't even convincing himself.

"Well, I hope so…for your sake," Jeff said. He turned his back to Scott and said, "You can leave now."

He might as well have said, "You're dismissed." Scott hated feeling powerless, having no choice but to take all this crap and disrespect. As Ant-Man, he was used to a certain lack of respect from his peers, but it was always in jest. It was different at work, being dismissed in such a callous and cold way by his boss. Since he needed his job, he had no choice but to suck it up.

Good thing he could become Ant-Man. That always made him feel powerful, the polar opposite of how he felt at work. It was also a great stress reliever.

Meanwhile, he did the right thing. He kept his emotions in check; he didn't snap and raise his voice, or say something he'd regret. Instead he said, "Thanks, have a great day," and dutifully left Jeff's office. He'd worked too hard to build an honest career for himself to throw it all away with a few careless words.

He went about the rest of his day, trying to stay focused. The strategy worked—he managed to forget about Jeff's disrespect and the whole order of protection situation. When his workday ended at six, he was looking forward to going home and having a normalish evening with Cassie. He picked up some Chinese for dinner. If she got her homework done early maybe they could kick back together, watch a movie on Netflix.

When he entered the apartment, he was surprised to see Cassie on her knees near the closet, as if searching for something. She stood quickly and said, "Hey."

He asked her what was going on, and she said she was just looking for her gloves, which didn't make much sense during a spell of beautiful weather in May.

Then she said the gloves were for some science project, involving ice. Scott sensed that something was off with Cassie, and he knew it probably had to do with the FBI. As a teenager, a lot of things made her self-conscious, so today those feelings must have intensified. He felt awful, knowing that she must've had a weird day at school with the federal marshal shadowing her. He said, "Sorry again for getting you involved in this."

She said, "No worries." Then she kissed him on the cheek and went into her room and shut the door.

He was proud of having such a laid-back, well-adjusted daughter. He'd put her through a lot in the past fourteen years, and it was amazing how well she'd handled it all.

They watched a movie after dinner, Tom Hanks' latest, and then they went to bed. In the morning, as usual, he was up first. He left a note for her on the kitchen table, "Have a wonderful day," and then left for work with Carlos escorting him.

It was another beautiful spring morning. As Scott walked toward the subway, he noticed a lot of ants on the ground—especially near trees and on lampposts, fire hydrants, garbage cans, and other objects. Perhaps this was because it was such a perfect day—ants liked their good weather, just like humans did—but then again, there had been a lot of nice days recently.

Scott arrived at work. He was about a half hour into his workday when Carlos came over and whispered into his ear: "We have a situation."

They went to a corner, out of earshot of the other workers, and Scott said, "What is it? Does it have to do with Dugan?"

"We can't locate your daughter," Carlos said.

Scott felt sick, and angry, and terrified—mostly terrified.

"What do you mean 'you can't locate her?'"

Carlos explained that Roger, the other marshal, had been waiting to escort Cassie to school. But she hadn't left the building that morning, and they hadn't been able to find her.

"What do you mean? She was in my apartment this morning."

As he was saying this, Scott realized he hadn't actually seen her.

"She's not in the apartment. We checked," Carlos said.

"It doesn't make any sense," Scott said. "You guys are staked out in front of the building twenty-four/seven."

"I just wanted to inform you what's going on," Carlos said.

"Well, thanks for the wonderful information," Scott said, already on his way out of the office.

Jeff wasn't going to be happy that he had to leave work early, but Scott didn't care. This was about Cassie now, and her safety was all that mattered.

In the cab uptown, Carlos tried to reassure him that it was highly unlikely that Willie Dugan was connected to this. But Scott feared the worst. Had he miscalculated this whole situation from the beginning? Maybe it had been cocky of him to pooh-pooh Dugan's potential threat to his family when the FBI believed the threat was real. After all, Scott hadn't had any contact with Dugan in nearly a decade, so did he know, truly, what Dugan's intentions were? Dugan apparently had murdered three people already, so why not kill a few more?

When the cab reached Seventy-Eighth Street, Scott rushed out in front of his building. Roger, the FBI agent who was supposed to have Cassie's back, was standing with George, the surly fifty-something Greek-American superintendent of the building.

Roger was finishing a cell call, saying, "...Okay...right...I'll get back—"

Scott interrupted. "You were supposed to be protecting her."

"He's here," Roger said into the phone. Then he ended the call and said to Scott, "Okay, calm down."

"My daughter's missing, and you want me to stay calm?"

"Are you sure she was in the apartment this morning?"

"You guys are staking out the place!"

"She didn't leave the premises," Roger said. "We would've seen her."

"Maybe she's in the building somewhere," Scott said. "Have you checked other apartments, the basement?"

"We checked everywhere," George said. "She's not here."

Scott resented George's tone. George sounded irritated and put out, the way he acted when he had to come fix a toilet. To him, someone's missing daughter was just an inconvenience that was complicating his day.

"You're gonna have to check again," Scott said. "What about the roof? Did you check the roof?"

"The door to the roof's bolted from the inside," George said. "No one went up to the roof."

"Check the roof," Scott said.

George reluctantly entered the building.

Carlos joined Scott and Roger.

"What about her school?" Scott asked.

"She isn't there, just checked," Roger said.

"We have to check again," Scott said.

"Hey," Roger said, "where are you—"

Scott didn't wait for him to finish. He took off in a sprint toward Cassie's school.

"Wait," Carlos called after him. "You can't go alone."

Scott was tired of this protective-custody crap. He wished he'd handled this alone, brought the fight to Dugan instead of waiting for the fight to come to him. If it turned out Dugan was involved in this—if Dugan hurt Cassie in any way—Scott would never forgive himself.

Scott went right to the main office and said to the first person he saw—a twenty-something blonde woman—"Is my daughter Cassie Lang in school today?"

"I don't do attendance," she said.

"Who does?"

"Barbara is away from her desk."

"When's she getting back?"

"Sir, you're going to have to wait."

"I can't wait. Can you just check?"

"Sir—"

Carlos had entered, gasping from the sprint over. Showing his badge, he said, "FBI. Do what he says."

The woman went to a desktop, pulled up the morning's attendance, and said, "No, she's absent today."

Scott cursed. He turned and kicked a desk, knocking off a plant; the pot smashed on the floor.

The principal rushed in and said, "What's going on here?"

Scott had met the principal, a squat, balding guy—Michael something. He let Carlos explain that Cassie was missing.

"How do you know she's missing?" Michael asked.

Scott was too impatient to deal with these questions. He said, "How do you know she's absent? Maybe there's a mistake. Can you call her teacher?"

The blonde woman went to make a call. Scott noticed several ants, in a line, marching across the floor. This wasn't unusual, of course.

Or was it?

He glanced toward the wall near the door and saw a couple ants there, as well.

"I'm sure there's some explanation," Michael said. "So this has to do with the protective-custody situation? Another agent talked to me yesterday."

"We're not sure what it's related to," Carlos said.

Scott looked across the hallway and saw a girl being escorted to the nurse's office by a female teacher. The girl had a bloody towel over her nose.

"I hope it's all okay," Michael said. "Sorry, it's been a crazy morning here today already, and the day's just beginning."

"Why crazy?" Scott asked.

"There was an incident in gym class," Michael said.

"What type of incident?"

Michael had a look that asked, *What difference does it make?* He said, "Appears to have been some sort of accident."

The blonde office worker came over and said, "I just checked with her homeroom teacher. She definitely didn't arrive at school today."

A thought was hitting Scott, a possible explanation for all of this, but he didn't want to go there. Not yet, anyway.

As he rushed out of the school, he heard Carlos calling out, "Hey, where're you going now?"

Scott returned to his apartment building.

Roger was in front. He asked, "Was she there?"

Scott walked right past him.

"The building has been under video surveillance, as well," Roger said, "so there has to be an explanation."

Heading up, two stairs at a time, Scott passed George, who was annoyed and sweaty, and said, "Not on the roof, just like I said."

Scott ignored George. He went into his apartment, right to the closet.

The boxes looked undisturbed, and the safe was locked. Maybe he was wrong about this. After all, how would Cassie have figured out how to open the safe? It had been manufactured in Germany, was one of the most secure home safes on the market, and he had never told the combination to anyone. Maybe this had nothing to do with the Ant-Man suit. Maybe Cassie had been telling the truth yesterday, and she really had been searching for her gloves in the closet.

But he opened the lock—and, sure enough, the suit was gone.

"No, Cassie," Scott said. "You didn't? Why? Why?"

He imagined the worst—Cassie getting injured or killed—and it would be his fault. He'd been working hard and trying to be a responsible dad, and he'd given his kid access to a suit that could shrink her to the size of an ant. What kind of parent was he? Did he even deserve to be a father?

But he could blame himself later—right now all he cared about was finding Cassie. If she'd put on the suit and figured out how to operate it, that could explain how she had bypassed the FBI agents. But Cassie wasn't practiced with the suit. She could be ant-sized now, on the loose somewhere in the school or in the city. And she could get herself killed.

He was going to head back to the school when he noticed a couple of ants on the wall near the closet. Was it possible that Cassie was somewhere in the apartment?

Scott was thoroughly terrified, on his knees, crawling around, searching for his ant-sized daughter, when he heard: "What is it?"

Roger had entered.

Scott considered telling Roger the truth. After all, the whole reason for keep his identity a secret was to protect Cassie. But now that she could be in danger, maybe he should take advantage of all the help he could get to find her.

He was about to blurt it out, tell Roger about Ant-Man, but he caught himself. He realized that if Cassie were the size of a fingernail it was doubtful the FBI, or anyone, could track her down any faster than he could.

"Just looking for my, um, keys," Scott said.

"Oh," Roger said, "I'll help you."

"No," Scott snapped. Then, calmer, he said, "I mean, I can find them myself, thanks. Actually, I just want to be alone for a little while, okay?"

"Sure, I understand," Roger said. "And just so you know, we put an APB out to the NYPD and federal law enforcement in the area. We'll locate Cassie soon, I promise you."

Scott thought, *Yeah, I hope you're all using magnifying glasses.* "I appreciate it, thanks," he said. "I'm sure she's just hiding somewhere. You know, playing hooky."

"I'm sure you're right," Roger said.

When Roger left, Scott resumed crawling around the apartment, saying, "Cassie? Cassie, where the hell are you?"

SEVEN

WHEN Cassie had heard the front door shut—meaning her dad had left for work—she went right to the closet, opened the safe, and took out the Ant-Man suit. She replaced everything in the closet to make it looked untouched, and then shut the door.

As she expected, the suit didn't fit her, but she had an idea. If the Pym gas shrank people, couldn't it shrink objects—like the suit itself? It was worth a shot.

Cassie opened the canister and pressed a metal lever. Nothing happened. She tried again, harder, and the suit suddenly shrunk to the size of a Barbie outfit. Wow, pretty cool, but now it was hard to find the lever. She did, with her fingernail, and pushed it the opposite way. The suit expanded, but it was still way too small for her. It took a lot of tries, but she finally got the suit and helmet to a size that fit her perfectly.

The helmet had antennae and an opening for her mouth, and a big round ant-like space to look out. Wow, this would be awesome to wear on Halloween. She'd been to a party once where some kid was in an Ant-Man costume. What if she went next Halloween as the real thing? She could make a bet, go, "I'll bet you a thousand dollars that I can shrink to the size of an ant," and then she'd actually do it. She could make a fortune in this thing, enough to buy any clothes she wanted. Forget H&M—she'd be shopping on Madison Avenue.

She was ready to shrink, but she was a little scared. She didn't think the suit could damage her body, or else her dad would be dead by now; but she'd always been afraid of things she'd never tried before. She reminded herself that she'd been scared to go zip-lining that time two summers ago and then then she did it and it wasn't so scary; it was actually fun. So she did what she always did when she was scared—closed her eyes and counted backwards from ten. Her pulse was pounding, but when she said "one," she bravely pushed the lever.

Nothing happened.

She didn't get it. She tried a few more times; still, nothing happened. Maybe to get the suit to work you had to do something else. There wasn't an "on" button or anything.

"That would be too easy, dad, right?" she said aloud.

There didn't seem to be any sort of activation switch in the helmet, either. There was a mesh-like part in the chin area. She blew into it, but nothing happened.

She tried to remember how her dad used the suit. She'd only seen him shrink himself a few times, and each time she'd been so awed by the sight of him suddenly becoming miniscule that she hadn't really paid much attention to anything else.

Her dad had only told her about his secret identity about a year ago. Mom had gone away to live in Oregon and Cassie was upset, crying a lot. Her dad took her aside and said, "Cassie, it's really important for me to be a good father to you. Actually, it's the most important thing in my life—my main reason for living. And part of being a good father is being trustworthy, and part of being trustworthy is being honest, so I want to be honest with you about everything."

She'd thought he was going to apologize to her for something, the way he was always apologizing to her mom for all of the bad stuff he'd done in the past. But instead, he said he had to tell her about a "big secret" he'd been keeping from her.

He told her about Ant-Man and Dr. Pym. He told her that he had the ability to shrink to the size of an ant while maintaining his proportional strength, and that he could communicate with other ants, and that sometimes he went on missions with other super heroes to fight evil in New York and around the world.

Of course she didn't believe him. She thought it was all just some story to make her feel better, like when parents tell their kids there is a tooth fairy. But then he said he'd show her, and he put on the suit. She still thought it was some kind of lie, but it was a lie she wanted to believe. What girl didn't want to believe that her dad was a super hero?

"Okay, ready," he said. "Stand back. And when I shrink, don't panic. I'll still be able to talk to you in my normal voice, and I can turn back to my normal size at any time. Are you okay? You promise this won't scare you?"

She still thought he was joking around. He'd say, "Whoops, it didn't work today, maybe next time"—but it would be okay anyway, because she knew it was just a fantasy. She wasn't expecting anything to actually happen.

But then he did it—right in front of her. He activated the Pym gas—she remembered that part—and an instant later, it seemed like he had disappeared.

"Cassie, I'm right here. Wave to me."

Then she spotted him on the floor—the size of an ant.

"Oh my god," she said, and crouched right over him so she could get a better look.

It was her dad, all right. And yeah, he was waving to her.

Now, as she continued to figure out some way to activate the Ant-Man suit, she started to feel ridiculous. Why was she doing this, anyway? Her dad would be so mad at her if he found out. Was it worth it just to get revenge on Nikki? That would feel great, but it wouldn't make Tucker McKenzie forget what he'd seen on Instagram— and it wouldn't get him to want to hang out with her, which was all she really wanted.

She was about to give up, to put away the suit, when she felt some lever-like thing in the sleeve above her left hand. There was one in the right sleeve, too. She pushed the left one up and felt a buzz in her body, like a small electric shock—kind of like when she was wearing a wool sweater and touched a metal doorknob on a cold day. She tried it with the other sleeve, and the same thing happened. It was weird and cool, but they were just little shocks; nothing seemed to be happening. It was probably just something to do with the material the suit was made from.

Then, just for the hell of it, she pushed both levers at once *while* releasing the Pym gas, and something definitely happened because suddenly all she could see was this huge grayish hairy thing. She reached out and touched it; it felt like a puffy dandelion. Wait, was the gray thing a *dust ball?*

She looked to her left and saw more gray stuff over something that looked like a big blue field. She knew that blue—it was her carpet.

"Oh my god, this is so freakin' cool," she said.

She took a step forward, and her legs felt normal. She wriggled her hands; they felt normal, too. Everything about her seemed normal—well, except that she was the size of an ant.

Then she tried to run. Big mistake. In an instant, she zipped across the entire rug in a blur and smashed into something—maybe the end table. It didn't hurt at all, though—whatever the suit was made of, it sure was strong.

She tried to run again, and this time she ran into a blur of white—probably a wall. She continued running around for a while, bumping into things and bouncing off as if she were the ball inside a giant pinball machine. It was like skiing or roller skating, she realized: She was going to suck at it at first, but she'd eventually get the hang of it. This was way more fun than any ride she'd ever been on at Great Adventure or Disney, or any video game she'd ever played. Why hadn't her dad ever told her how awesome being Ant-Man was?

Cassie laughed and, though it sounded like her normal laugh, she wondered whether people would be able to hear it. Could people hear her voice at all? There were a lot of things she needed to figure out about this, and it was definitely more fun than going to school.

She wondered what would happen if she jumped.

Bad idea.

She leaped what she thought would be a foot off the ground, but instead she catapulted into the air and smashed her head against the ceiling. Again, though, it didn't hurt at all, and it was way more fun than it was scary.

After several minutes of darting and jumping around the apartment, she already felt more in control of her movements. Also, weirdly, she was able to see objects clearly when she focused on them, kind of the way a telescope can zoom in. She didn't know how she was able to do this, as she wasn't pressing any buttons or levers. It seemed as if she was doing it all with her mind.

She could've stayed in the apartment all day and had a blast, exploring her abilities, but there was a reason she'd put on the Ant-Man suit. It was time to get going.

She crept under the door—this was so awesome; she didn't need keys anymore!—and went to the top of the landing. She counted, "One, two, three..." and jumped.

It was perfect—well, almost perfect. She hit her destination at the bottom of the landing, on the fourth floor—but then she bounced off the wall, hit the ceiling, and tumbled down the next staircase. She screamed like she was on a roller coaster until she landed on the second floor. She was totally fine, but she decided to take the stairs one by one down to the ground floor.

She slipped under the vestibule door, zipping over a copy of *The New York Times,* and went outside. Out on the street, she saw legs in front of her. She looked up and zoomed in on Roger, the FBI agent, who was waiting to take her to school.

Trying out her voice, she said, "Hey! Hey!" But Roger had no reaction. He didn't seem to hear her at all.

Having fun, Cassie jumped up in front of Roger's face and said, "See ya later, dude!"

She was laughing, but he had no idea. He must've thought she was a fly or a gnat or something because he swatted her with his hand and muttered, "Get!"—she could hear *him* clearly—and she fell on top of a garbage can.

"Hey, that wasn't nice," she said. Then she jumped onto the sidewalk and headed toward First Avenue.

That's when she saw all the ants.

She'd seen magnified images of ants in books and online, but nothing could have prepared her for the gigantic-looking bugs. They looked like aliens. Scary aliens.

"Oh my god, gross," she said. Then she said, "Please...please stay away from me, okay?"

Was she really talking to ants, expecting them to understand her?

Now the ants were coming from everywhere, like an invading army. She was ready to turn back the other way and run, but she was outnumbered—they would swarm her.

But it quickly became obvious that the ants had no intention of hurting her. She wasn't getting any kind of menacing vibe—and maybe she'd already gotten used to how they looked close up, because they didn't look scary anymore, either. If anything, they seemed scared of *her,* or at least in awe. They formed lines around her, watching her the way people come to watch the president, or some other famous person, pass by in a parade. She felt loyalty, respect, even love from the ants.

Another weird thing: From such a close vantage point, all the ants looked different. She used to think that all ants looked alike, but now she could see that, just as humans had different features that set them apart from one another, so did the ants. They had different size eyes, antennae, legs, coloring, even facial expressions. There were kid ants, teenage ants, adult ants, and older, wiser grandparent-like ants. There was a sense of community, order—just like with humans.

Cassie slowly walked past the ants, feeling so different than the way she felt at school, especially lately. She remembered how Nikki and her friends had laughed at her yesterday during lunch. Sometimes at school, she felt like no one really cared about her. Yeah, okay, she had a few good friends—but even Nikki, someone she thought was her best friend, had turned on her. If you couldn't trust your best friend, who could you trust?

But strangely, Cassie trusted these ants—more than she'd trust any human except maybe her dad. She felt respect from them, knew they'd always have her back. The ants made her feel confident, important.

Now she couldn't wait to get to school and get on with her plan.

She kind of jogged up the street, afraid to go too fast—First Avenue wasn't far away, and she didn't want to shoot off into traffic. She had to pass over leaves, twigs, gum, candy wrappers, spit, dog poop—she still had a human-like sense of smell, that was for sure—and other gross-looking stuff. Some things looked so weird up close, she wasn't sure what they were. She hadn't seen any other insects yet, and she definitely wasn't looking forward to meeting a cockroach or water bug—that would be super scary. She did pass a dog on a leash, though, which was unbelievably awesome. It was this little teacup poodle that looked as big as five elephants.

She'd been trying to avoid people, and she continued to stay away from the huge feet as she turned onto the First Avenue sidewalk. She was afraid someone would step on her, but she wondered what would happen if someone did. She didn't think she'd get squashed—if that were true, her dad would've gotten squashed like a million times already.

Then, sure enough, a gigantic-looking boot—probably a Timberland—came down on her, and everything went dark for a second. She felt trapped, as if she were in a tiny room and the lights had suddenly gone out. Part of the shoe was pressing against her head, but amazingly it didn't hurt at all. Then, as if nothing had happened, the person passed by and Cassie was totally fine.

Whoa. If she was strong enough that a maybe two-hundred-pound man stepping on her didn't do any damage at all, just how strong was she?

Well, why not find out? At the next corner, she stopped in front of a metal garbage can, which of course appeared to be gigantic. She reached out with one of her tiny hands and pushed the metal. It was like trying to knock down a building—but, sure enough, the garbage can toppled onto the street, all of the trash spilling out.

The rush was amazing. She felt like the most powerful person, or insect—whatever she was now—in the world. No wonder those ants were lining up, showing her so much respect.

Cassie darted under the doors of Eleanor Roosevelt High School. She saw some other ants here and there—watching with curiosity, or maybe awe—as she passed by. She zoomed in on a clock and saw it was a little past nine—which meant it was time for gym class. This was perfect!

The gym was on the second floor. Going up steps, she realized, was trickier than going down. She jumped from step to step, which got kind of tiring. There had to be an easier way to crawl up the stairs—or along the wall, the way ants did—but she didn't have time to experiment.

She made it to the second floor and ran down the hallway toward the gym, again passing some oncoming shoes and other objects. Then she saw Mr. Griffin, her math teacher, talking to another teacher. Cassie stopped and listened in on some of their conversation. They weren't talking about anything interesting, just some TV show they'd both been binge-watching—but it would be so cool to follow her teachers around all the time, and her classmates, too, to hear all the things they talked about when she wasn't there. It was like being invisible, but so much more awesome.

She would've loved to find Tucker McKenzie, spy on him all day, and find out what he really thought about her. But she knew she didn't have a lot of time. Roger had probably figured out she was missing, and it wouldn't be long before they called her father. She had to get home and put the Ant-Man suit back in the safe before her father figured out that she'd taken it.

In gym, all the kids were lined up for a basketball drill to practice layups. Cassie sucked at basketball—she was glad she was missing this. She spotted Nikki in line, talking to Keely, one of Nikki's friends.

"I don't know. I don't want to," Nikki said

"Come on, it'll be so much fun," Keely said.

"Yeah, maybe, I don't know," Nikki said.

"You'll change your mind," Keely said.

Cassie had no idea what they were talking about. She would've loved to listen in on the rest of the conversation, wait for them to say something juicy, but she didn't want to waste any time. So she jumped onto the back of Nikki's waistband—which seemed gigantic, of course. Then, grabbing onto the gym shorts with both hands, she leaped off—as if she were skydiving off a mountain—holding on to the elastic the whole time. Sure enough, the shorts came down, and Nikki was left standing in her panties in front of everybody.

Nikki was shocked and confused. She made it worse for herself by screeching, so soon all the kids in the gym were looking over at her and laughing. Cassie was laughing, too. She leapt off the elastic just as Nikki was yanking her pants back on.

"Oh my god, why did you do that to me?" Nikki asked Kelly.

"What?" Keely said. "I didn't do anything."

The gym teacher—Coach Jill, who was always strict and kind of nasty—came over and said, "What's going on here?"

"Keely pulled down my shorts," Nikki said.

"I did not," Keely said.

Nikki and Keely continued to bicker about it, and Jill warned them that they would have to sit out the rest of the class if they didn't behave. Meanwhile, Cassie and the other kids in the gym were still laughing. Too bad Tucker McKenzie wasn't there—that would have been so perfect.

Coach Jill blew her whistle, and the basketball drill continued. Then Cassie had another idea. There were a bunch of basketballs off to the side, not far from the basket where Nikki was practicing. Cassie moved behind a ball, which looked as huge as a Ferris wheel to her; when Nikki approached the basket and was about to shoot a layup, Cassie threw it at her. Cassie only meant to freak Nikki out and make her miss the shot. But Cassie still had a lot to learn about controlling her strength and movements as Ant-Man, or Ant-Girl, or whoever she was. She winged the ball much harder than she intended, and it smashed into Nikki's nose. She heard a loud crunch.

Nikki was screaming and crying as blood gushed from her nose onto the gym floor. Coach Jill hadn't seen what had happened, but assumed Keely was involved and shouted at her to go to the principal's office. She instructed another kid, Julien, to go get the school nurse. Then Coach Jill tended to Nikki, trying to calm her down. She told the other kids to leave the gym and go to the cafeteria.

Cassie felt awful. She hadn't meant to actually hurt Nikki—she'd just wanted to scare her a little.

"Oh my god, I'm so sorry," she said, and then she saw what looked like a huge blob of blood coming toward her. She darted out of the way before the blood reached her—that would have been so gross.

Then panic set in. All this time, since she'd gotten the idea to borrow the Ant-Man suit, she'd been so excited about seeing the world from the point of view of an ant and discovering all these cool powers that she hadn't really thought about the possible consequences. She'd hurt Nikki, probably broken her nose, but what if she'd done something even worse? She just wanted to go home and put away the Ant-Man suit before anyone found out—or she caused even more trouble.

She darted across the gym floor, past the school nurse who was rushing to Nikki's aid, and then continued along the hallway, going along the wall to stay out of the way of the crowd of students. At the end of the hallway, she saw Tucker McKenzie and stopped.

She recognized his sneakers first, his orange-and-blue New York Knicks-colored Nikes, and then she looked up at his face. Even from this weird angle, he was unbelievably cute. He was obviously talking about what had happened in the gym. "Who did it?" he asked, and another guy said, "Nobody knows," and another guy said, "Somebody was sayin' the ball just flew up and hit her all by itself," and then Tucker said, "Man, that's so crazy."

Cassie zoomed in on Tucker's face. No wonder she had such a big crush on him. He was the hottest guy she'd ever seen.

Then the Nike came down on top of her, and she was wedged into a gap in the bottom of the sole. She was trapped again, like being in a dark jail cell. She wasn't scared, though—just frustrated.

"Come on, move, Tucker," Cassie said. "I gotta get out of here."

Finally, after maybe a minute, Tucker walked away, probably heading to his next class. Cassie went down the stairs, ran toward the front of the school, skidding as she turned, and then exited.

She ran along First Avenue, avoiding obstacles like before, and then she saw her dad—and Roger behind him—running toward the school. Had her dad found out about the Ant-Man suit? She was going to be in such big trouble—the most trouble she'd ever been in.

She crossed the streets, noticing more ants out, and made it back to her apartment building. She jumped up the stairs, step by step, as fast as she could. Her father was looking for her at school, and when he didn't find her there, he'd come back home. She had to turn back to normal size and put away the Ant-Man suit before that happened. Finally, she made it to the fifth floor. She saw George, the building super, coming toward her.

He seemed angry about something. He stopped walking and looked down, his gaze zeroing in on her. This was the first time since she'd shrunk that a human had looked right at her, and this huge face staring at her was terrifying. Then he grimaced and said, "Damn bugs," and his huge-looking black shoe was coming down fast toward her. He was trying to squash her.

She missed his shoe—which seemed to make the whole floor shake—by an instant. She was afraid that if he got a good look at her he'd realize that she wasn't actually a bug. She slipped under the door to her apartment to safety.

Well, sort-of safety. There was still that minor step of returning to normal size. She pressed the little levers in her sleeves simultaneously, figuring this would do the trick, but nothing happened. She tried pushing them in the opposite direction, but nothing happened.

"Please," she said. "Come on." She was starting to panic, afraid she'd never be able to return to normal size again.

She maneuvered the levers every which way, but still nothing happened—not even the buzzing sensation like before. She just wanted to get out of the suit, but she was afraid to, at this size. She wanted to be strong, to not cry, but her lips were quivering and a few tears dripped down her cheeks.

The front door opened, and her dad entered. He looked gigantic, but she was getting used to seeing people from this angle.

"Dad!" she called out. "Dad, I'm over here! Daddy!"

He couldn't hear her, of course. She felt like she was in one of those frustrating dreams, where you want to do something or get somewhere but you keep getting distracted, or aren't fast or strong enough, and the thing you want to do never gets done. Except that this wasn't a dream—this was a full-blown nightmare.

Her dad went right to the closet, checking the safe, so he must've somehow figured out that she'd taken the suit. That was a good thing, she realized, because he would try to find it. Sure enough, he dropped down on his hands and knees. She yelled, "Dad, over here! Over here!"

And then Roger entered the apartment. Her dad made up an excuse that he was looking for his keys and managed to get Roger to leave him alone.

"Cassie? Cassie, where the hell are you?"

She'd never heard her dad sound so upset.

"Here, Daddy!" She was jumping, waving her arms. "Right here."

She ran right in front of him, and he saw her.

"Cassie. There you are."

He held out his giant hand, and she jumped into it. Then he lifted it up toward his face. His eyes were glassy, bloodshot.

Yeah, she was in big trouble all right.

Huge.

EIGHT

SCOTT was thrilled, angry, and terrified. He was thrilled that he'd found Cassie, angry that she'd put him through a morning of hell, and terrified that he'd never be able to restore her to normal human size.

"For god's sake, Cassie," he said, looking down at his miniature daughter in the palm of his hand. "Why did you do this? Why?"

He didn't expect her to respond. It was difficult to figure out how to modulate your voice in the Ant-Man suit; it was impressive enough that she'd figured out how to shrink and get around. She was a smart kid, but she was also fearless—a dangerous combination.

"Never mind," he said. "I'm sure there's a reason, but I don't care about that right now. I just want to help you, do you understand me?"

He could barely see her head, but he could tell she was nodding,

"Good. Now I'm going to put you back onto the floor, and I want you to do exactly what I tell you, okay?"

Again she nodded.

He rested his hand on the floor, and she jumped off. This was his baby, the most important thing in his life, and she was about half the size of a pencil eraser. As a father, he'd never felt so powerless.

"Don't worry, everything's going to be okay. I promise."

But the thing was, he had no idea whether everything would be okay. He was in uncharted territory. He'd never had to explain to anyone how to use the Ant-Man suit, and the only one who'd taught him was Hank Pym. But Cassie was a teenager, she was still growing, and she was a woman. He had no idea how these variables would affect the technology.

"Okay." His voice was trembling, but he couldn't help it. "You need to activate the expanding gas. What I want you to do is touch those control levers in the sleeve. You found them already, I'm sure, but what you want to do this time is hold them down for a count of five and, at the same time, bend your head down with your chin against your neck. Okay, on the count of five. One, two—"

Something slammed into Scott like an uppercut to the jaw. He catapulted backwards and crashed into the closet door. It took a few seconds to orient himself and realize that he'd been hit by the helmet of the Ant-Man suit as Cassie returned to human size.

Scott was dazed, but managed to get up. He grabbed her arms and said, "Cassie, are you okay? Say something to me. *Please.*"

"I…I'm fine, Daddy."

He could tell she was scared. Her calling him "Daddy" got to him. Always did; always would.

"Thank god." He hugged her as tight as he could without hurting her and said, "You have no idea how worried I was."

"I—I'm so sorry. I'll never do anything like that again. I—I swear, Daddy."

He lifted off the helmet and shook her. "Are you okay? How do you feel?"

"I feel totally normal. I mean, like, physically."

"Are you sure? Every organ in your body, including your brain, shrank and expanded again. Who knows what effect that could have on you?"

"I know, but I'm totally fine, I swear."

"Where were you born?"

"*What?*"

"What city were you born in?"

"San Francisco."

"What was the name of your first dog?"

"Duncan. I told you, I'm fine, Dad."

"I hope so. I seriously hope so."

"What're you so worried about, anyway?" Cassie asked. "You do this all the time, right?"

"Yes, but I'm an adult," Scott said. "You're still growing. I have no idea what effect this could have on you. It's uncharted territory, and it's dangerous, and it's nothing you should've done on your own."

"I feel normal," she said. "Just a little stupid, I guess."

Now that he knew that she was okay, and apparently unharmed, Scott's anger was kicking in.

"Why did you do this?" he said. "The suit isn't a toy, Cassie. I've told you that how many times? I thought I could trust you."

"You *can* trust me."

"Can I? You haven't done a great job of proving that to me today. What if I didn't find you? What if somebody else found you? What if you got injured or killed? Didn't you even think about that?"

"Honestly, no," she said.

"See, that's the problem. You can't live your life this way! You can't be a risk-taker. Risk-takers wind up dead."

Scott knew he was being hypocritical, of course. For most of his life, he'd been a huge risk-taker and adrenaline junkie.

But that was him. This was different. This was his daughter.

"I just wanted to play a prank on somebody," Cassie said.

"A prank?" he said. "What kind of prank?"

"I know how stupid it's gonna sound now," she said, "but I was angry and...well, I didn't actually expect it to work."

"So this prank was on me?" Scott asked.

"No, somebody at school."

Scott remembered seeing the ants at the school and the girl with the broken nose in the nurse's office.

"Wait," he said, "did you hurt somebody?"

"Not intentionally," Cassie said. "I just wanted to throw a basketball at Nikki and—"

"What if somebody saw you? You were small, but you weren't invisible."

"Nobody saw me."

"Trust me, somebody always sees something. Especially nowadays. So now they think a basketball, all by itself, hit Nikki in the nose? What if somebody filmed it on their phone? It could be all over Instagram or YouTube now, going viral."

"Nobody filmed it. They think this other girl Keely did it."

"And what happens when Keely denies it? This isn't something to joke around about. There are serious consequences, especially right now when we're under an order of protection."

"It's not *all* my fault," Cassie said.

"What do you mean? How do you—"

"If it wasn't for you, none of this would've happened," she said.

"You're the one who has the stupid Ant-Man suit, you're the one under the protection order. You're the one with all the secrets—I just have to keep them for you."

Cassie was crying. Scott hated seeing her get so upset. Besides, she had a point.

"Okay, you're right," Scott said. "I was just scared, that's all. You mean everything to me. I don't know what I'd do without you."

"I—I'll never do it again." She was sobbing now. "I promise. I promise."

Scott held her, swearing that everything would be okay, and that they'd put all this behind them.

Then, when she was calming down, he said, "So...how did it feel to be Ant-Man?"

"Unbelievable," she said.

"I know, right?" Scott said.

"I mean, you used to tell me stories about about how cool things look, like from that perspective, but until I saw it for myself I had no idea. And the strength—"

"Yeah, it was the same way when I was Ant-Man the first time," Scott said, remembering the day Hank Pym had showed him how to use the suit. "I'm still amazed you figured out how to move, get around. It took me a week to get used to it."

"I don't know, I guess it just came to me naturally," Cassie said. "Um, but by the way, it's Ant-Girl, not Ant-Man."

Scott smiled. Cassie went on, describing how she'd learned to run and jump, get up and down stairs, and her experiences observing the behavior of ants. Scott chimed in with anecdotes about how he'd learned to speak in a normal-sounding voice, even while ant-sized, and how he'd learned over time to communicate with ants. As upset as he was at Cassie for stealing the suit and putting herself in danger, he had to admit it was invigorating to talk to her about her experiences. Other than Hank Pym, Scott had never talked to anyone who'd experienced this, and the fact that he could talk about this with his daughter made it even cooler. He'd always felt closest to her when they were doing something techie together, building something or taking it apart—but lately, since she'd become a teenager, they hadn't been as close. It was nice to have another thing to bond with her over.

"Can I do it again sometime, Dad?" Cassie asked.

"Maybe," Scott said, "when you're twenty-one. And you're going to have to figure out some way to make this up to Nikki."

"How?" Cassie said. "I can't tell her the truth."

"No, but you can make it up to her karmically," Scott said. "You can send her a get-well card, help her with her studying, do something nice for her."

"But Dad, she's been so mean to me lately," Cassie said. "That's why I wanted to get revenge in the first place."

"Well, you're going to have to find another way to work out your differences," Scott said. "Oh, and you're grounded. No going out with your friends at all. You can only leave the apartment to go to school, and after school you come right home."

"This isn't fair."

"After what you did today, you're getting off easy. And you can have your phone with you at school for safety, but no phone at home for a week."

"No phone?" Cassie was shocked. "That's insane. I can't survive without my phone."

"For thousands of years, humans figured out how to survive without iPhones. I think you can too."

As Scott helped Cassie take off the rest of the suit, he could tell she was upset. That meant he'd gotten through to her. He was getting good at this whole single-dad thing; maybe the self-help books were starting to pay off. Cassie needed a little good old-fashioned tough love, and Scott was giving it to her.

Scott away put the suit in the safe and said to Cassie, "I'm changing the combination, so don't even think about getting in there again."

"Don't worry, I won't," Cassie said.

"I believe you," Scott said. "Now we have to give Roger and everyone who's looking for you an explanation for what happened this morning. The whole NYPD is looking for you."

"Oh my god," Cassie said.

"I have an idea," Scott said. "Let's go."

Scott and Cassie went outside, in front of the building, where Roger, Carlos, and George were conferring. Roger and Carlos were obviously relieved to see Cassie.

"Where was she?" Roger asked.

"On the roof," Scott said.

"I checked the roof," George said. "Nobody was there."

"She was hiding," Scott said.

"She couldn't have been on the roof," George said. "The door was bolted from the inside."

"You must've made a mistake, 'cause that's where I just found her," Scott said.

George said, "I didn't make a—"

"It doesn't matter now," Roger said. "She's safe, that's the important thing." He said to Carlos, "Call off the search."

Carlos went to make the call.

Roger said to Cassie, "Why did you do it? You want to scare everybody?"

Before Cassie could answer, Scott said, "She was upset about the protection situation."

"I understand that," Roger said, "but we're here to help her and help you. You're putting all of us in danger if you don't let us do our job. We want to give you your privacy, but if we have to stay in the apartment from now on, we will."

"That won't be necessary," Scott said. "Cassie and I just had a long talk about it, and I got her assurance that it won't happen again. Isn't that right, Cassie?"

"Yep, that's right," Cassie said. "I promise."

Roger stared at Scott, then at Cassie, for a couple of beats. Then he said, "Right then. Well, I guess we should be getting to school now, shouldn't we? Better late than never."

"I'll go get my backpack," Cassie said, and raced back into the building.

Carlos returned and said to Roger, "Taken care of." Then he asked Scott, "So you want to head back to your office?"

"Let's do it," Scott said.

He was eager to get back into a routine and forget about this crazy, frantic morning. He noticed that the ants he'd seen earlier were gone. They'd obviously been intrigued by the presence of a new person, a girl, in the Ant-Man suit. But now the hoopla was over, and they could get back to their busy work routines as well.

Carlos had parked across the street. As Scott was getting into the car, he saw a very attractive, Mediterranean-looking woman—long, dark hair, tight business suit—walking toward him along the side-walk. They noticed each other at the same time and smiled. Mutual attraction? Well, at least Scott thought so. Too bad he had an FBI escort, or he would've said hi to her, tried to strike up a conversation.

As Carlos drove away, his cell chimed. He took the call on Blue-tooth, saying, "Yeah."

Scott could tell by Carlos's ultra-serious expression that he was receiving some sort of important information.

Scott was looking back at the woman, wishing he'd said something to her.

To whomever was on the line, Carlos said, "Yeah…okay…right… okay…thanks."

Then he ended the call and said, "That was about Willie Dugan."

"You got him?" Scott asked.

"Better than that," Carlos said. "He's dead."

NINE

CARLOS explained that Willie Dugan's body had been found in an abandoned warehouse in Breaux Bridge, Louisiana.

"Good news for you," Carlos said. "Looks like your life's about to go back to normal, man."

"Louisiana?" Scott was surprised. "What was Dugan doing down there?"

"Who knows and who cares?" Carlos said. "I'm just happy he's off the board, aren't you?"

"How did he die?"

"I didn't get any details yet," Carlos said. "This news is probably ten minutes old, but I'm sure we'll all hear more soon. With any luck, by the end of the day the protection order will be lifted and you and your family can go on with your lives."

The end of the protection order would certainly be great news, but something about this gave Scott an uneasy feeling. On his phone, he searched for information about Dugan. There was nothing online about his death, though this made sense since the story was just breaking. It would be all over the news soon. Scott was eager to hear about the details.

"What's up?" Carlos asked. "I thought you'd be excited about this."

"Defense mechanism," Scott said. "I don't like to get too excited or upset about anything until I have all the facts. Saves me from feeling the letdown when things don't work out the way I want them to."

"Ah, I get it," Carlos said. "But sometimes you gotta let loose, be optimistic. Dugan's dead, man. Hallelujah."

Carlos drove Scott directly to the job site on Park Avenue South. A tech startup from San Francisco was opening its New York offices, and Scott and his crew from NetWorld were installing all of the networking and cabling for the full-floor office. It was such a complicated job, coordinating the install for the 150-user network, that he practically forgot a federal marshal was shadowing him. Like, well, an ant, Scott got absorbed in his work and in his daily routine.

At the end of the workday, Carlos came over to Scott and said, "Ready to roll?"

"What's up with Dugan?" Scott asked.

"There's been a complication," Carlos said. "Well, hiccup's a better word. Dugan's body hasn't been ID'd yet. But don't worry, it's him."

They walked through the office, along an aisle between the empty cubicles.

"I don't get it," Scott said. "How is this possible?"

A few workers were nearby. Scott could tell that Carlos didn't want to talk about it right now.

But when they were back in the car, heading to the Upper East Side, Carlos said, "Some of this hasn't been made public yet, so this is between me and you right now, okay?"

"Understood," Scott said. "What's going on?"

"It's definitely a murder case," Carlos said. "Maybe somebody in Dugan's own crew got to him, but he made an enemy somewhere.

His body was found in a container with some kind of acid. So the ID'ing might take a while."

"And why are they so confident it's him?" Scott asked

"Cops found his clothes and ID at the scene," Carlos said. "Also a car nearby, stolen, had his prints all over it."

"Still, how do they know it's him?"

"Look, I'm not directly involved in the investigation, so I can't give you all the answers," Carlos said. "All I know is what I've been told—Dugan was in that container."

Scott wasn't convinced. There were too many loose ends.

"I can tell you still have that defense-mechanism thing going on," Carlos said. "Don't worry, you'll have closure soon. It's all good, man."

WHEN they arrived at Scott's building, agents Warren and James were in front, conferring with Roger, the other marshal. When the men saw Scott and Carlos pull up, their conversation ended.

"What're they doing here again?" Scott asked.

"Not my department," Carlos said. "My job's to protect you. I wouldn't sweat it, though. It's probably just a routine follow-up."

Scott approached the men with a fake smile. "Welcome back, guys. Long time, no see."

"We need to talk," Warren said.

He sounded all business, not like he was here for a "routine follow-up."

In his apartment, Scott saw that the door to Cassie's room was shut. He heard the soft beat of music leaking out.

"Have you heard the news?" Warren said.

"Some of it," Scott said. "Maybe you can fill in the blanks."

"What do you know?"

Scott didn't want to mention anything that Carlos had told him in confidence, so he said, "Why don't you start?"

"Willie Dugan was found dead today in Louisiana," Agent James said.

"And you're positive it's Dugan?" Scott said.

"Why don't you tell us?" James asked.

"Tell you what?" Scott said. "You're the ones filling me in."

James and Warren exchanged looks.

Then Warren asked Scott, "Have you had any recent contact with Willie Dugan?"

"Are you seriously hitting me with this again?" Scott asked.

Deadpan looks said they were.

"No," Scott said. "I have not had any contact with him in years, I told you that. I have no idea what he was doing in Louisiana, or who killed him, if that's your next question."

"Who said he was killed?" Warren asked. "I just said he was dead."

"Your marshal told me, okay?" Scott said. "He didn't give me any details, but it's probably in the news, too, and I don't appreciate you showing up here, accusing me, when I obviously, absolutely have nothing to do with any of this."

Unfazed, Warren asked, "Did you have contact with any of Dugan's associates?"

"What?" Scott asked.

"Have you?" Warren asked.

"Of course not," Scott said.

"I hope you're telling the truth," Warren said. "You have a daughter who depends on you."

Scott got the implication, but he asked, "What's that supposed to mean?"

"Means it would be a shame if you had to go back to jail for a long stretch," Warren said.

Scott, raging inside, managed to keep his cool exterior.

"Why would I be in touch with anybody?" Scott asked.

"Seems obvious to me," Warren said. "Dugan has a grudge against you, you think he's coming after you, so maybe you decided to beat him to the punch. You're an ex-con, after all, long rap sheet, and you probably have connections. Maybe you hired somebody to track him down and take him out. The way it went down, it certainly looks like a revenge killing."

"I want a lawyer," Scott said.

"Only guilty people need lawyers," Warren said.

"No, innocent people who are being harassed need lawyers," Scott said.

Warren fake-smiled, then nodded to James. They headed toward the door.

When Warren was near Scott, though, he stopped. Looking right into Scott's eyes, he said, "I know when somebody's hiding something, when somebody has a secret—and you're one of those guys. I don't know what you're hiding, but, trust me, I'll find out." He paused, then added, "We'll be in touch," and left the apartment.

Eager to find out the latest, Scott turned on the TV news. Sure enough, the discovery of the body in Louisiana was the lead story on CNN, but there were no new developments as far as Scott could tell. The police believed that Willie Dugan had been killed, perhaps by a member of his own crew. The lead detective on the case gave a brief press conference, stating that the investigation was "ongoing," but he didn't offer any new information.

Scott was concerned; he didn't like when he had more questions than answers. If Dugan had been rubbed out by a crew member, why go to such lengths to dispose of the body—making it difficult or even impossible to ID—but leave behind articles of clothing and a car with fingerprints? If the objective was to cover up the murder, why not get rid of everything?

It was possible that whoever had committed the murder simply wasn't very bright. After all, most of the criminals Scott had encountered weren't the sharpest tools in the shed, which was why they usually wound up in jail. Scott hoped that was the case this time and that Dugan was dead, but he wasn't getting his hopes up just yet.

Cassie came out of her room and asked, "What's going on? What were you talking about with those FBI guys?"

Scott shut off the TV. He hoped she hadn't overheard the conversation, specifically the part when Agent Warren had threatened to send him back to jail. He didn't want to frighten or upset her.

"Oh, actually it's good news," Scott said. "They think the protection order is going to be lifted soon."

"Wow, really?" Cassie said. "That's so awesome. Is that all you were talking about?"

Cassie probably hadn't overheard the conversation, but she was a bright kid with good intuition.

"Yeah," Scott said.

Scott was a terrible liar. He had a feeling Cassie knew he was holding something back.

But if she did, she didn't push it. "That's really cool," she said.

"That Roger guy isn't so bad, but it will be a relief to be on my own again."

Scott managed to forget about Dugan for a little while and he enjoyed a relaxing evening at home with Cassie. He was thrilled that she was showing no adverse effects from her experience in the Ant-Man suit. She seemed totally normal—healthy, happy, and full of energy.

Throughout the day, Scott had gotten a couple of texts from his ex, Peggy. She was still, understandably, upset about the protection situation. He'd written her that he expected the protection order to be lifted, but hadn't given her any details.

At around midnight, she called and said, "Why is the marshal still outside my house?"

Bracing himself, Scott and said, "I'm sorry, I was hoping it would be over by now."

"I can't take it anymore," she said. "They follow me everywhere."

"I know," Scott said. "But it won't be for much longer."

"Why is it still going on? I saw on the news—Dugan's dead, right?"

"Presumed dead," Scott said. "But the FBI seems confident that it's him."

"What if it's not him? What if this goes on forever?"

"It won't," Scott said.

Peggy breathed deeply.

"Can I speak to Cassie please?" she asked. "I called her, but her phone's off."

"She went to sleep early," Scott said.

"I miss her so much," Peggy said. "How has she been?"

There was no way Scott was going to tell her that Cassie had put on the Ant-Man suit and shrunk herself. Scott knew Peggy would use it as proof that he wasn't doing a good enough job with his parenting.

"We had a little issue here, discipline-type thing, but it's all cool now."

"Is she okay?" Peggy sounded panicked.

"Fine," Scott said. "Better than ever. I think she has a boyfriend."

"Tucker McKenzie," Peggy said matter-of-factly.

"You know about him?" Scott asked.

"Of course I know about him," Peggy said. "There are things a girl will share with her mother that she won't share with her father, you know."

Scott didn't like the sound of this at all.

"What exactly are these things you're referring to?" he asked.

"They haven't even kissed yet, if that's where your mind's going," Peggy said. "But your daughter's getting older now, Scott. You're going to have to accept that."

"You mean my daughter, Rapunzel?" Scott asked.

Peggy didn't laugh. It had been a long time since she'd laughed at one of his jokes.

"I feel like I'm missing out on these moments," Peggy said. "I mean, by not being there."

"You'll see Cassie this summer," Scott said. "It's only a couple of months away. Meanwhile, you're where you need to be, with your mom. How's she doing, by the way?"

"Not good, I'm afraid," Peggy said. "Some days she doesn't recognize me. Well, most days."

"So sorry to hear that," Scott said. "If there's anything I can do, let me know."

"Thank you, I appreciate that," Peggy said. "And I'm sorry I got so upset with you before. I had a bad day with my mother and everything, and it was wrong to take it out on you. I want to thank you…for taking such good care of Cassie while I'm gone. I know you only want the best for her. We're both lucky to have you in our lives. I don't know what we'd do without you."

Scott didn't know where this sudden tenderness was coming from, but he liked that she wasn't blasting him for the protection order anymore.

"That's nice of you to say," he said.

"I mean it," she said. "I know I haven't been there for her lately, but she's lucky to have a father like you. You've really stepped up to the plate, Scott, and you never have to worry. I'll never tell anyone about you-know-what. That's in the vault forever."

Scott knew that "you-know-what" meant his identity as Ant-Man.

"Thank you," Scott said. "That means a lot to me."

This was refreshing—having a normal, amicable conversation with his ex-wife. Wouldn't it be great if it were always like this? If they didn't have bitterness, hidden agendas, and underlying aggression built in to every interaction? Maybe they'd still be married.

"You're a good man," she said. "That's one thing about you I've never doubted."

IN THE morning, Scott made Cassie her favorite breakfast: French toast. Then, after making sure that Roger knew Cassie was actually in the apartment this morning, Scott and Carlos left for another day of work.

Scott was getting used to having Carlos around. For years, Scott's life had centered around Cassie and his work—as Ant-Man and at his nine-to-five job—so he hadn't had much time to develop new friendships. Carlos was a good guy from the Bronx, and had been with the FBI for twenty years. He was happily married and had two kids—a boy who'd just graduated from Fordham, and a girl a couple of years older than Cassie.

In the car, they made small talk about all the changes in Manhattan over the past twenty years. Carlos told Scott that the edginess of New York had almost disappeared, and now there seemed to be the same drugstores and banks on every corner.

"How'd you wind up in New York?" Carlos asked.

They were driving down Second Avenue now, moving slowly in traffic approaching the Ed Koch Bridge.

"I like cities," Scott said, "and I've always wanted to be in Manhattan."

This was partly true. He did like cities, but he probably would have stayed in San Francisco, or at least in the Northwest. He'd come to New York because Tony had offered him a job at one point. Also, it made the most sense for Ant-Man to be in Manhattan, the center of it all.

"But why the Upper East Side, man?" Carlos asked. "You're not some stuffy business guy. I see you living farther out—Brooklyn, or maybe Washington Heights. But the Upper East Side?"

"I used to live downtown—Lower East Side, Ludlow Street—but then Cassie got into high school up here, and I wanted to make life easy for her. She's had a tough life. You know about my past, and then there was a lot of moving around, with the divorce. I'm just looking to give her some stability for once. I think that's important."

"Cool, man," Carlos said. "You love your daughter, I respect that. With me it's the same way. Hurt me all you want, but you touch my daughter, there's gonna be hell to pay. This protection situation has been hard on you, but I heard through the grapevine that the M.E. has a DNA sample and should make an official announcement about Dugan's death sometime today."

"Well, that's great news," Scott said.

They passed the bridge, and traffic started moving steadier. Scott would be at the office soon, which was great because he wanted Jeff to see that the order of protection wasn't affecting his work—or at least his ability to get there on time.

"Hey, I have an idea," Carlos said. "When this is all over and done with, you and I should go out sometime, get a couple of beers, watch a game. Or I'll invite you up to the Bronx, take you around to some places in my neighborhood. Show you how real New Yorkers live."

Ten years ago, Scott had been a felon, working with Willie Dugan, and now he was making plans for a boys' night out with a federal marshal? And, oh yeah, he was also Ant-Man. How things had changed.

"Yeah, I'd like that a lot," he said.

AFTER another long, absorbing day at work, Carlos drove Scott home. As they were getting out of the car, Scott spotted the dark-haired woman he'd seen yesterday. She was coming toward him, and she smiled when she noticed him noticing her.

Not wanting to miss another chance to talk to her, Scott said to Carlos, "Hey, can you give me a little privacy here?"

"Sure thing," Carlos said. "*Buena suerte,* bro." He went across the street.

"Hey, excuse me," Scott said to the woman.

She stopped near Scott, looking even prettier up close. She was dressed casually in jeans and a thin black leather jacket, and she had her black hair back in a ponytail today.

"I think I saw you the other day," Scott said.

"Don't worry, you weren't imagining it," she said.

"Wow, you remember?" he asked.

"It was only yesterday. If I forgot already, I think I'd have some serious memory issues, wouldn't I?"

"You never know," he said. "Sometimes you see somebody and you see them again and you don't make the connection. You see somebody at work, and ten minutes later you see them on the street and think, 'Who is that? Do I know you?' It happens to me all the time."

"But it didn't happen this time, right?" she asked.

She was funny. He already knew he liked her.

"Nope, not this time," he said. "I'm Scott."

"Jennifer," she said.

"Jennifer," Scott said, "I've always loved that name."

"You have?"

"No," Scott said. "I was totally lying about that."

She laughed. After the date from hell with Anne, it was nice to meet a woman with whom he seemed to actually connect from the get-go.

"But it is a beautiful name," Scott said.

"Thank you," she said. "I think Scott's a horrible name."

She remained deadpan for so long Scott thought she was serious. Then she laughed and said, "Got ya."

"Yes you did, yes you did." Scott was smiling. "So do you live in the neighborhood?"

"Yes, actually. Just moved here from Hoboken. How about you?"

"I was downtown, moved up here in the spring. I live right over there." He pointed toward his building. Carlos was standing there, looking at something on his cell phone.

"Nice," she said. "So, um, who's your friend?"

"Who?" Scott really was lost for a few seconds. "Oh *him*. He's just my, um, driver."

"Your driver?" she repeated.

Scott, in his work clothes—jeans and a hoodie—didn't exactly look like he had a driver.

"Yeah," Scott said, "I'm not wealthy, but I've always wanted a driver, so I hired Carlos. Some dreams do come true, right?"

Scott waved to Carlos, and he waved back. Jennifer waved at Carlos, too.

"So," Scott said to Jennifer, "do you want to get a coffee?"

"Right now?"

"Yeah," Scott said. "I mean if you don't have another plan, we can go to the diner right around the corner."

"Um, well..." She hesitated, looking at her phone.

"Or another time," Scott said. "Maybe we can exchange numbers. Or if you just want to consider this a drunk dial, we can go on with our lives."

She smiled, then said, "Actually, I think I have time for a coffee right now."

"Great," Scott said. "Let's do it."

They went around the corner to the Green Kitchen, a diner on First Avenue, and sat in a booth toward the back. Scott, facing the street, saw that Carlos was hanging around outside. This protection thing was seriously cramping his style as a single guy in the city, but he was proud of himself for coming up with that story about having a driver. It had even sounded mildly impressive.

They ordered coffees and talked about their jobs. She was a freelance photographer and also did graphic design. Scott told her about his work in computer networking.

"How did you get into that?" she asked.

"I've always loved building things," he said. "It started with the usual: model airplanes and cars when I was a kid. And when I was bored, I loved to take computers apart and put them back together."

"That's amazing." She sounded genuinely impressed.

"It's something I can do with my daughter. She's fourteen, just started at the high school around the corner."

"You have a teenage daughter?"

"Are you about to compliment my youthful good looks?" Scott asked with smirk.

She laughed, then said, "I have a daughter myself, actually. She's also fourteen and lives with her father part of the time. She goes to that high school, too."

"El-Ro?"

"What?"

"Eleanor Roosevelt? It's the name of the school."

"Oh, yeah, right. Yes, that's the one."

"Wow, this is very cool," Scott said. "I mean that we have daughters the same age. I wonder if they know each other. My daughter's Cassie. What's your daughter's name? I'll ask her if she knows her."

"Oh, my daughter hasn't started there yet," Jennifer said. "She still goes to school in Hoboken, but she's starting at this new school next week. Her name's Rebecca."

"Wow, great," Scott said. "I'll tell Cassie to look out for her."

In addition to learning that they had daughters the same age, Scott was thrilled to hear that Jennifer had an ex-husband—that they were in similar places. If this worked out, it could be perfect. They lived in the same neighborhood, could get together all the time. She seemed witty and interesting; if their daughters hit it off and became friends, that would be even better.

Then Scott saw the ant crawling along Jennifer's napkin. Was this the story of his life or what? Just when things were going well, when there was the potential for something good and stable to happen in his life, something came along and messed everything up. Usually that thing was an ant.

"So when did you decide to become a photographer?" Scott asked, trying to distract Jennifer so she wouldn't notice the ant. Wait, make that *ants.* Yep, there were two of them now—the other one was crawling along Jennifer's spoon.

As Jennifer went on, talking about a photography class she'd once taken in college, Scott tried to send the ants a message to go away and give him some space. This had never worked when he wasn't in his Ant-Man suit, and it didn't work this time, either. Worse, a third ant had appeared on the table. It was only a matter of time before every ant living in every nook and cranny in the restaurant would come out to say hi. Normally Scott loved this, but not when he was trying to hit it off with a woman.

"I love taking pictures," Jennifer was saying. "I guess I've always been visual that way." Then she saw the ants on the table and said, "Oh my god."

Here we go again, Scott thought. If she wanted to kill the ants, he'd have to defend his little friends—and then she'd get pissed off, think he was some kind of weirdo, and storm out of the diner, and that would be the end of another great date.

But she didn't flip out. Instead, her expression brightened, and she said, "Wow, so cool."

Surprised by her reaction, he said, "You're not grossed out?"

"No, I think ants are amazing. Don't you?"

"Yeah, I do—but I've met a lot people who don't feel that way."

"I know, it's crazy," she said. "Like, why are people so anti-ants? It doesn't make any sense. I've always loved ants. When I was a kid, I used to stare at the ant colonies in our backyard for hours. Their behavior, how organized they are, is amazing, and they have no idea we exist. It makes you wonder if something bigger than us is out there watching. It seems logical that we're like ants, and there are other levels of civilizations—life, whatever you want to call it— that're more complex than our civilization, but we're just not aware of it. I guess ants can teach you a lot about faith. I'm sorry—I'm rambling, I know, but do you get what I'm saying? You're probably thinking, 'Who is this crazy woman? Why did I invite her to have coffee with me? How can I get out of here without insulting her?'"

"So ants in a diner really don't bother you at all?" Scott asked. "I mean, you don't see them as a sign of uncleanliness?"

"What? No," she said, as if that concept baffled her. "This is New York City. Ants are cleaner than most people who ride the subways."

"I bet that's actually true," Scott said. He smiled. He liked Jennifer's eyes. They were grayish-blue. He wanted to say something about them, but he'd just met her, and he feared it would come off cheesy. What would he say? *Your eyes, they're so beautiful?* He didn't want to be *that* guy.

"Your eyes, they're so beautiful," he said.

He wished he could suck that one back in.

"Thanks," she said. "I was just thinking the same thing."

"Really? I think you're just saying that."

"No, it's true."

"What do you like about them?"

"The color," she said. "I don't think I've ever seen that shade of blue—they're very arresting. And I love the depth. Some people's eyes seem one-dimensional. You look at a person, and you don't need any more information. But your eyes have layers, they tell a story. When I look into your eyes, I see a little boy with a big secret."

More great eye contact.

Then she said, "It's interesting, isn't it?

"That we both like each other's eyes?" Scott asked.

"No, that the ants only seem to be around our table. Look, there's another one." She looked at the wall next to Scott where a large ant was crawling. "And there's another." There was a smaller ant on the saucer beneath the coffee mug.

Afraid that their waiter, or someone else at the diner, would see the ants and try to kill them, Scott put out his napkin. While Scott couldn't communicate with ants outside of his suit, the ants were able to sense danger on their own. They also knew that Scott was a friend, so all the ants on or near the table wisely and obediently crawled onto his napkin.

"Wow, the ants seem to like you," she said. "I don't think I've ever seen anything like that."

"Eh, it's not such a big deal," Scott said.

He released the ants safely onto the floor, where hopefully

they'd avoid any ant traps or insecticide and make it safely back to their nests.

"Oh shoot." Jennifer was looking at her iPhone. "I was supposed to meet my daughter at a friend's downtown, and she's waiting for me right now. I have to jump into a cab."

Scott wondered whether this was just an excuse to get away from a bad date. He'd used various incarnations of the "there's a family emergency" story himself when things seemed to be going nowhere on a date. Maybe he'd read too much into her comment about his eyes. Maybe the ant conversation had weirded her out, after all.

"I'm really having a great time, and I wish I didn't have to take off," she said. "But I don't want to keep my daughter waiting."

"Totally understandable," Scott said. "I know how teenagers can be."

She opened her purse and said, "I should give you some money…"

"Stop. It's on me," Scott said.

She thanked him. As they left the diner, Scott noticed that Carlos was across the street now, but Jennifer didn't seem to notice him.

"Thank you again," she said.

"No, thank *you*," he said, and he leaned in and kissed her on the cheek.

His stomach tightened, and his heart sped up. Scott had fought alongside the greatest super heroes in the world, battled the most dangerous villains, and—when he shrunk in his Ant-Man suit— was, pound for pound, the strongest of them all. But asking a woman out on a date still scared the hell out of him.

Mustering up the courage, he said, "So…we should, um, do this again sometime…I mean maybe go for dinner or to a movie sometime.

I mean, only if you're up for it. You don't have to decide now. I mean, it's okay if you don't want to—"

"No, I'd like that very much," she said.

Thinking, *Whew*, Scott said, "Great, let's exchange numbers."

She gave him her cell number, and he called it.

"Perfect, got it," he said.

"See you soon," she said. "And tell your driver I said hi."

Scott smiled, watching her walk halfway up the block. *Man, what a woman.*

Then he headed home in the other direction.

CARLOS insisted on escorting Scott up to his apartment to make sure everything was safe and secure. Cassie was in her room, doing her homework, and nothing seemed out of the ordinary.

"I think I can handle it from here," Scott said.

"Cool," Carlos said. "You know the drill. If you or Cassie gotta go anywhere, text Jimmy, the marshal who'll be out there tonight. If the protection order isn't lifted by then."

Carlos and Scott shook hands.

"Seriously, I appreciate everything you've done for us," Scott said, "and thanks for hanging back and giving me some space before."

"Hey, guy's gotta help a guy out, right, hombre?" Carlos said. "Besides, it's been a long time since I've been single. I'm living vicariously through you, man."

After Scott cooked dinner—okay, yeah, he microwaved a frozen pizza and heated up some frozen carrots and peas, but it was still a meal—he texted Jennifer:

> Had a great time, thank you for being so
> spontaneous! Let's hang out this weekend, dinner
> and/or a movie. Looking forward to it!

He couldn't remember the last time he'd been so excited about a potential girlfriend.

As he cleaned up and did the dishes, he saw the usual ants crawling near the sink and fridge. Usual, because he'd seen and come to recognize most of them; as Ant-Man, he had communicated with the ants who lived in the apartment building. He knew that most of them lived in a colony in the wall behind his kitchen sink, and that they considered the apartment a safe haven in a building—well, an entire world, to the ants—full of poisons and enemies. Among their enemies were other city bugs—cockroaches, water bugs, silverfish, etc—but most of these bugs knew enough to stay away from ants, sensing the collective power of the smaller insects. When other bugs occasionally strayed into the apartment, Scott was kind to them, capturing them and freeing them outside, or even feeding them. Yes, he was aware that feeding cockroaches was an activity that most of society frowned upon. But since he'd become Ant-Man, he had learned to admire and respect all insects.

He checked his phone—no response yet from Jennifer. It would be great if they went out again and hit it off, and this evolved into an actual relationship. Scott was happiest when he was in a stable relationship, but he hadn't been in one since the first few years of his marriage. Who was he kidding? Since the first few *months* of his marriage. And it would be great if Cassie had a positive female role model in her life—even a step-mom, eventually.

Later in the evening, he was sitting at the edge of his couch/bed, looking at his phone, when he heard:

"Hey, I'm not gonna have to read that text out loud, am I?"

Cassie was near her room and had just finished brushing her teeth.

Scott smiled, realizing that he was acting like the teenager in the household.

"Haha, got me," he said. "Goodnight, Sweetie."

"Goodnight, Daddy."

She kissed him on the cheek and went into her bedroom.

Scott watched the TV news—nothing about Willie Dugan, or an official identification of his body. In international news, Cap and Natasha, the Black Widow, had busted a Hydra heist in Thailand. Whenever Scott heard about the achievements of other super heroes, he couldn't help feeling a pang of jealousy—the way he'd feel if he were an athlete watching a game in which he couldn't participate. He knew he had his place in the order of things, but sometimes he hated being on the sidelines. He wanted to be in on the action, making the big plays.

On the TV, a reporter at the scene explained how the town had been liberated. A stock photo of Natasha was shown, providing an additional source of angst for Scott. She and Scott had had a little fling during a mission in France a few years ago. Natasha had made it clear from the get-go that this wouldn't be anything serious, and Scott had thought he'd be up for that. Let's face it, she was way out of his league—she was way out of everybody's league. But call him a hopeless romantic, he couldn't help getting emotionally attached. So yeah, he felt hurt when she took off one morning without even leaving a note. But Scott knew it was probably for the best. He didn't know whether he was really into Natasha, or the idea of Natasha—a free spirit with no kids, no roots. She could pack up and go whenever she wanted. It was part of what made Scott feel different from most super heroes. He was a parent first and a hero second, and while he envied guys like Tony and Cap, he knew that type of lifestyle wasn't for him. Being a dad was his most important role, and he wouldn't give it up for anything.

"Bye-bye, Natasha," he said, and flicked off the TV.

Yeah, he didn't need yet another complicated, emotionally unavailable woman in his life, no matter how hot she was.

But Jennifer the photographer—Scott was already falling asleep—now *she* made sense.

IN THE morning, Scott still hadn't heard back from Jennifer. He didn't think it was such a big deal—some people didn't text right back. But when he still hadn't heard back by noon, he started to wonder whether he'd ever hear from her again.

He'd thought she meant it when she said she wanted to see him again, but maybe the thing with her daughter had been a blow-off, after all. Maybe Scott had misread her interest in ants, and he'd freaked her out. Or maybe the stuff about having a driver had sounded odd to her, especially with Carlos lurking outside the diner. Some women felt put on the spot at the ends of dates, and said yes to getting together again when they really just felt awkward saying no.

At lunch at a bagel store around the corner from the office, Carlos asked Scott what was going on with the woman from yesterday.

"Nothing yet," Scott said, checking his cell. There still was no text from Jennifer, but he'd gotten one from Peggy asking him whether there was anything new about Dugan.

"Don't fret, bro," Carlos said. "Good thing you live in New York and not Kansas."

"I don't know what that means," Scott said.

"I'm just saying, don't worry—there's a lot more ladies out there. You'll meet somebody else."

"But there are a lot of women in Kansas, too," Scott said.

"I know. It was just a joke," Carlos said.

"If it's a joke, say Siberia, or Antarctica—someplace where there really aren't a lot of women. Not Kansas."

"Wow," Carlos said. "You really liked this girl, huh?"

"What?" Scott said, then realized how he was behaving. "I'm sorry, man, I didn't mean to jump down your throat. Yeah, I guess she did get into my head a little. There was something about her, you know? But, yeah, you're right. I'm not in Kansas."

"You mean Antarctica," Carlos said, smiling.

Scott was absorbed in his work for most of the day, trying to finish the final installs on the job and get the last group of users up and running. He wasn't thinking about Jennifer, but then he impulsively texted her:

Hope you're having an amazing day!

As soon as he clicked send, he regretted it. If she didn't want to go out with him again, getting another text wasn't going to change her mind. And if she wanted to go out with him and just hadn't gotten around to texting him yet, this additional text wouldn't exactly help his cause.

"Whatever," Scott said to himself. "It's all good."

But then he got a reply:

invalid number

Hmm—that was weird. Scott hadn't gotten the response after sending the previous text. So unless there was a glitch in the cellular network—probably unlikely in this case—Jennifer had discontinued her cell service.

Or there was another possibility: She could have blocked his number. He didn't think he'd said or done anything that could've offended her so much that she'd actually block him. Or had he? Collecting ants on a napkin and setting them free onto the floor of a public restaurant wasn't exactly behavior that a lot of people considered normal. He'd thought she was one of the exceptions, that she "got it," but apparently he'd misread her.

Oh well, it was out of his control now. He got back to work on the install. Then Carlos entered.

"We gotta go," he said. He grabbed Scott the way a Secret Service agent would grab the president and pull him out of harm's way.

As Carlos was pulling Scott through the office, workers stopped to watch. Scott felt just as confused as they looked. "What's up? What're you doing?"

Carlos didn't answer. He seemed tense and wouldn't make eye contact.

"Come on, you're freaking me out," Scott said. "What is it? Will you just tell me? What happened? Is it Dugan?"

Carlos waited until they were alone, on the elevator heading down to the lobby. Then he said, "It's Cassie."

"What is it?" Scott's pulse was pounding. "She didn't show up for school again?"

He was ready to get angry at *her*. Had she gotten into the safe, put on the Ant-Man suit again? He'd changed the combination, so he didn't see how it was possible, but she was a clever kid—sometimes too clever.

Carlos looked away, as if searching for the right words, then looked right into Scott's eyes and said, "She was abducted, Scott."

TEN

CASSIE had decided she didn't like Tucker McKenzie after all. Yeah, he was incredibly cute and awesome, but a lot of boys were incredibly cute and awesome, and it didn't matter how incredibly cute and awesome a boy was if he was going to be a jerk and totally change and act all cool around his friends just because of something he saw on Instagram.

So the day after Cassie had hit Nikki in the face with the basketball, Cassie decided she would ignore Tucker. Sometimes in the hallway after drama when she'd see him, he'd say "Hey" or "What's up?" and she'd say "Hi" or "Hey" back. But this time when she passed him and he said, "Hey," acting like the whole Instagram thing hadn't even happened, she ignored him, didn't even make eye contact, and kept walking.

But weirdly, ignoring him seemed to make him more into her. The next day Cassie was leaving Gotham Pizza on York with a couple of friends, and Tucker was there with his friends. Tucker had never said anything to her before, or even noticed her, when he was with friends. But this time he said, "Hey, Cassie, yo, wait up."

Cassie's friends went ahead back to school, and Tucker's friends walked away, too. Tucker and Cassie were alone, face-to-face for the first time ever.

"Are you like mad at me for something?" Tucker asked.

Playing dumb, Cassie went, "What do you mean?"

"I don't know," Tucker said. "You've just been, like, cold to me lately, that's all. The last couple days, I mean."

Cassie was trying not to think about how incredibly freakin' cute Tucker was—what with his smile and wavy brown hair—and how badly she wanted to kiss him.

"I just wanted to say," he said, "about what you posted on Instagram—"

"I didn't post it," Cassie said. "Nikki did, and it was wrong of her to do that because it was just a text, intended for her, and yes I wrote it, but I'm not going to be embarrassed and ashamed about it anymore. It was just a stupid text, so what? I had a feeling at the time—a feeling that just like came to me—and I wrote my friend about it. At least I thought I was writing my friend about it. And I don't care what you or anyone else thinks. You have no right to laugh at me like it's a big joke. It was humiliating enough to have something that I didn't want anyone else to see suddenly out there to be seen by everybody."

"Whoa, slow down," Tucker said. "I can't keep up with you."

Cassie *had* been talking fast—she did that a lot when she was nervous.

"Sorry," Cassie said, "but whatever. It doesn't matter now, anyway."

"For the record," Tucker said, "I was never laughing at you. I didn't even know about the Instagram thing until this morning, and I was flattered."

"You *were?*" Cassie said. "But I don't get it. When I saw you the other day, you were totally laughing."

"Must've been about something else, something that was actually funny. I don't think posting other people's texts is cool at all."

Was it possible that Cassie had made a mistake? She'd been so upset and humiliated, it was possible she'd jumped to a conclusion about Tucker. Great—she'd already been feeling bad about putting on the Ant-Man suit and accidentally breaking Nikki's nose; now she had something else to feel bad about.

"Oh, wow," Cassie said. "I had like no idea."

"It's cool," Tucker said. "Hey, do you want to go Carl Schurz one day? I can't till next week 'cause I have an SAT prep class and lacrosse practice, but next week would be awesome. I mean, if you're into it."

Carl Schurz was a park uptown. Was she asleep and dreaming, or was Tucker McKenzie asking her to hang out with him?

"Wait, this isn't part of the joke?" Cassie asked. "If I say yes, you're going to start laughing at me."

"I promise you, I won't laugh," he said.

It was cute; he seemed nervous, like he was afraid that *she* would reject *him.*

"Okay, then yes," she said. "I'd love that."

They walked back to school together—actually *together.* She had fantasized about walking somewhere with Tucker so many times, and now it was happening. The fantasy was real.

"Can I ask you a question?" Tucker said.

Was he going to ask to hold her hand?

"Of course," she said, hoping her hand wasn't too sweaty.

"Who's that old dude following us?"

"Old dude?" Cassie was confused.

"I think I've seen him around school, too," Tucker said.

Cassie looked back at Roger, trailing them about half a block behind. Cassie had been so absorbed, she'd forgotten about Roger.

"Oh, *him*," Cassie said. "If I tell you, can you promise to keep a secret?"

"Of course," Tucker said.

"Well, you might get totally freaked out, but he's an FBI agent—a federal marshal—who has to follow me around for some reason I don't know, and even if I did know, I wouldn't be allowed to tell you about it." Ugh. Cassie was talking fast again, probably making a fool of herself—she couldn't help it.

"You serious?" Tucker asked. "He's really with the FBI?"

"I'd never lie to you about anything," Cassie said.

"That's so cool," he said.

"That I won't lie to you or that I have my own FBI agent?" she asked.

"Both," he said.

At school, Cassie wished she didn't have to say goodbye to Tucker. She wished they were already in the park, and there weren't any other people around.

"See ya later," he said.

She went to her next class, drama, but she didn't know why she was bothering. She knew she wouldn't be able to focus on anything except Tucker McKenzie and how this was definitely the happiest day of her life.

THE NEXT day, Nikki was back in school for the first time since her nose had been broken by the basketball. She had a big bandage taped around her nose, and Cassie felt awful. She remembered what her dad had told her, how she had to figure out a way to atone for her sins with Nikki. Well, he hadn't said "atone" or "sins," but that had been the gist of it. Her dad was always telling her that you get what you give in life, which was kind of annoying. Especially because he was right.

Cassie couldn't muster up the courage to say anything to Nikki during homeroom, but afterward, she walked up to Nikki in the hallway and said, "Hey, I heard about your nose. I'm really sorry."

"What are you sorry for?" Nikki said. "It's not your fault."

Cassie flashed back to herself—ant-sized—winging the basketball at Nikki's face.

"Yeah, I know that," Cassie said. "What I mean is I feel bad it happened to you. Does it hurt?"

"When it happened it hurt like hell," she said. "Yesterday it still killed, but the doctor gave me some painkillers, and it's not so bad when I take them. Today it just hurts, but at least it doesn't feel like my whole head's about to explode."

"That sucks," Cassie said, "Maybe I can like help you do your precalc homework sometime."

"What do you mean?"

"I mean after school sometime, or over the weekend, I'll help you with precalc. I mean, I know you hate math, and you said your parents were even thinking you should get a tutor. And since math comes easy to me, I thought...I'd just be happy to help you, that's all."

They were at the end of the hallway, near the stairs. Kids passed by, laughing and talking without noticing them.

"I don't get it," Nikki said. "Why are you being nice to me?"

"No reason," Cassie said. "Just because."

"But there's no reason to be nice," she went on. *"I'm* the one who should be nice. When I was at the hospital, getting my nose looked at, I thought about what I jerk I was to you. And it's weird, but I thought maybe I like *deserved* to have that basketball break my nose."

"You didn't deserve it," Cassie said. "It was just an accident."

"No, it wasn't an accident," Nikki said. "It happened by itself. I know this is gonna sound crazy, but the ball just flew up from the ground and hit me in the nose all by itself. No one threw it at me."

"But Keely hit you with the ball," Cassie said. "I mean, that's what I've heard people saying, anyway."

"No, that's what Coach Jill said happened," Nikki said, "so of course the principal and the dean believed her because she's the teacher. But Coach Jill's lying—she didn't see anything. Even Keely herself said she didn't throw it at me, but the principal said I'm just denying it to protect Keely, which is so untrue. If she hit me with the ball, I'd say she hit me with the ball, I'd want her to get in trouble for it, but she didn't hit me with the ball, the ball hit me all by itself. I know it sounds crazy, because I feel crazy even saying it, but that's what happened, and it's so incredibly frustrating that nobody believes me. Everybody thinks I'm crazy. Even my own parents think I'm crazy."

Nikki was crying, the tears dripping down the bandage on her nose.

"I don't think you're crazy," Cassie said.

"Everybody thinks I'm crazy," Nikki said. "Everybody who was there and everybody who wasn't there."

"I believe it happened," Cassie said.

"You do? You're not just saying that?"

"No. I know you, and if you say it happened, then it happened."

"But how did it happen? It's crazy."

"Who cares?" Cassie said.

Nikki stared at Cassie for a few seconds, as if trying to figure out whether she was serious. Then she hugged her and said, "Wow, thank you. You're amazing."

Cassie was happy, too—it was great to have her best friend back.

"Hey, you want to go shopping on Eighty-Sixth Street after school?" Nikki asked.

"I'd love that, but I can't today," Cassie said.

Nikki turned for a moment and looked toward the end of the hallway where Roger was lurking, and then she turned back. "What's up with that guy, anyway?" Nikki asked.

"Oh, he's just nobody," Cassie said.

"Zoe said you told her he's a school supervisor?" Nikki sounded confused. "Has he been following you around every day? What's a school supervisor?"

"Yeah, he just like monitors student performance, you know, like a school performance monitor," Cassie said, knowing this didn't make any sense. Then she added, "I mean, it's like a school-survey-type thing. You know, research for the Board of Education—it's no big deal. Oh, wow, I have to get something from my locker before next period. Text you later."

Cassie had gotten away this time. But she knew it was going to be hard to keep Roger and the whole protection thing a secret from Nikki and everybody else for much longer, especially since she had already told Tucker about it.

Cassie had her best day at school in a long time. It felt great to be getting along with Nikki again, to not have a big vendetta on her mind. Now that Nikki was being so cool and nice, Cassie could barely remember why she'd decided to harass her in the Ant-Man suit the other day; in retrospect, it had been such immature, non-fourteen-year-old behavior, especially since there had been no reason to get even because Tucker wasn't actually making fun of her. Nikki posting that text on Instagram had probably helped Cassie, because it let Tucker find out that Cassie liked him, which he might have never known otherwise.

Cassie was so happy that even Roger following her around everywhere didn't seem so embarrassing or uncool anymore. She saw Tucker a couple of times—the first time, he was with friends by his locker and didn't see her. Then she saw him in the hallway where she usually saw him, and instead of just saying "Hey" to her, they had a whole conversation. Well, maybe not a conversation, but they talked for maybe thirty seconds, and he said he liked the shirt she was wearing, which was awesome because she'd decided to wear the shirt—the one from Uniqlo—specifically in the hope that she'd see Tucker today and he'd notice the shirt and comment on it, and now it was like a dream come true.

It was hard to focus for the rest of the day because she was so absorbed in replaying every second, every detail of her conversation with Tucker. A few times, teachers called on her in class, and she was lost and didn't answer. One teacher—Dave, her chemistry teacher—talked to her after class. He asked her whether there was something bothering her lately, and whether the "situation you're in"—meaning the protection order—was distracting her from her school work. She told him no, everything was fine, and that she'd be more focused tomorrow. But the truth was, all she cared about was Tucker McKenzie and what he would say to her, what she would say to him, and—most important—how it would make her feel.

Leaving school at a little past three o'clock, she hoped she'd accidentally run into Tucker. Well, it wouldn't be an accident—she knew he would probably be out front—but she didn't see him. She walked up the block and turned onto First Avenue, hoping she'd see Tucker there, when she saw the two men coming toward her.

At first she didn't think anything was so weird about it. The men were rushing toward her and seemed very serious, but this was New York City. There were tons of people here and tons of weird things going on all the time. Maybe the guys were just in a rush and weren't really coming toward her, just trying to get *by* her.

Then she saw that both men had guns, but she didn't have time to be shocked or even scared—and, besides, the whole thing seemed totally surreal. It was only when one guy, the taller guy, fired the gun—not at Cassie, at someone behind her—that panic hit, but by that point it was too late to react, because the shorter guy had grabbed her and was forcing her into the back of a car. A woman—someone on the street—yelled, "Hey, over there!" and Cassie was thinking, *Roger, oh my god Roger,* but the big guy was already in the car next to Cassie, and he slammed the door, and the car sped away.

Before Cassie could scream for help, the shorter guy put something over her face, a towel or a rag. It was wet and had a strong, sweet odor. She struggled and screamed into it, "Let me go, please, please," but he was still holding the rag over her mouth and nose, and she was getting spacey. Then she thought, *Oh no, it's like a movie, the stuff on the rag is making me pass out.* She was feeling more dazed, maybe partly from panic; it was taking a lot longer than in the movies, but it was happening, it was definitely happening, but why? Why her? She knew it had to do with her father, with the reason for that stupid order of protection. She remembered asking her dad once why he wanted to be Ant-Man, like what he got out of it, and he had told her, "There are good and evil people in the world, and the evil people deserve to be punished." Well, maybe she was an evil person, and she was being punished for what she'd done to Nikki, breaking her nose, and she was getting spacier from the stuff, knew her thoughts weren't making much sense, but she kept thinking, *Why? But why?* And when she tried to yell for help again, she couldn't even get her mouth to move.

And then everything went black.

ELEVEN

ABDUCTED? What the hell do you mean, abducted? What's going on?"

Scott and Carlos were in the elevator of the office building on Park Avenue South.

"It just happened," Carlos said, "around the corner from her school."

Scott was suddenly dizzy, lightheaded. He said, "This is a mistake, right? You mean you just can't find her?"

"No, she was abducted. Roger's been shot. But people got the plates, descriptions. We'll get her back, I promise."

Knowing this wasn't like last time, that this was real, Scott asked frantically, "Is Cassie okay? *Is she?*"

"As far as we know, yes."

As far as we know.

It was Dugan; it had to have been. Scott couldn't remember ever feeling so terrified, so helpless. It was the exact opposite of the way a super hero should ever feel—but most super heroes didn't have missing daughters.

"I guess that wasn't Dugan's body in that factory," Scott said. "I guess you guys messed that up, too."

"We don't know whether or not it's—"

"He's alive," Scott said. "You and I both know that."

They exited the elevator when they reached the lobby. Scott grabbed Carlos by the shoulders and pushed him back against the wall. "I need to know exactly what happened. Right now!"

"I told you all I know, man. A car pulled up. Somebody shot Roger and took your daughter."

"You were supposed to be protecting her," Scott said. "That's what this is all about. Can't you guys do your damn jobs?"

"Something went very wrong...obviously," Carlos said. "Our man is down. I'd suggest you let me go."

Knowing there was no time to waste, Scott loosened his grip and rushed out of the building with Carlos. They got into Carlos's Charger and, with the siren and strobe on the roof, made it to the Upper East Side in less than ten minutes.

In the car, Scott didn't say anything. He was clinging to the slim hope that there had been some sort of misunderstanding, after all. He wasn't ready to consider the possibility that Cassie was in danger, or worse. He hated feeling powerless, like a victim. He needed to be powerful, in control. He needed to be Ant-Man.

Any hope of a misunderstanding vanished when they approached First Avenue on Seventy-Sixth Street. The whole area had been cordoned off, and traffic was not being allowed through.

Scott exited the car. Behind him, Carlos said, "Hey, wait, where you going?"

Scott sprinted ahead, then weaved through the crowd until he reached the cordoned-off area near the avenue.

Scott had lifted the police tape and was about to duck under when a burly NYPD cop with a full-on Brooklyn accent said, "Hey, guy, you gotta get back."

"She's my daughter," Scott said. "Cassie...the girl who was abducted."

The FBI agent, Warren—the one who had come to his apartment the evening this whole nightmare began—was rushing toward them.

"It's okay," Warren said. "Let him through."

Behind the tape, Scott said to Warren, "Was it Dugan?"

"We don't know yet for sure," Warren said.

"Look, this is my daughter," Scott said. "My daughter, okay? I don't want your watered-down info. To hell with your protocol—*you* let this happen. I want to know what's going on in Louisiana and here. Right now!"

"Look, I understand how upset you are," Warren said, "but I've told you everything—I'm not holding back anything. As far as I know, the investigation into Dugan's death in Louisiana is still going on. Rest assured, I'm doing everything I possibly can to return your daughter to safety."

"Safety." Scott sneered. "You're doing a great job with that. What about witnesses? Anybody see anything?"

"Yes," Warren said. "They're still being debriefed, so there may be more info, but witnesses saw two men. One man shot Roger, and then they took Cassie. We have a preliminary ID on one of them, Ricky Gagliardi."

Scott hated the way Warren had said "they took" Cassie. It sounded so unemotional.

"I know Gagliardi," Scott said. "He worked with Dugan. That means Dugan's involved."

"Not necessarily," Warren said. "Dugan's guys could be working on their own. What do you know about Ricky Gagliardi?" Warren was suddenly interested only because—it was so clear now—his ass was on the line. Things had gone to hell on his watch. He wanted to find Cassie, all right—because it was the only way to save *his* job.

"I don't really know him," Scott said. "It was years ago—we know some of the same people."

Scott wasn't being entirely truthful. He knew Gagliardi, or "Gags," pretty well, having pulled a few jobs with him and Dugan. Gags was a big dude, a musclehead. Nobody dared mess with him, which made him a valuable asset when the crew needed to intimidate somebody. Scott didn't remember too much about Gags, but he didn't recall hating the guy. For a criminal, Gags had a decent enough personality. He loved to pull pranks—part of the reason he had the nickname "Gags"—and he was a big movie buff, used to talk about Scorcese flicks a lot. He'd always seemed to like Scott—had laughed at his jokes, anyway. Scott never had a falling out with Gags, never testified against him, and this is what he does ten years later? How does a guy go from laughing at your jokes to kidnapping your daughter?

"What about the car?" Scott asked. "Anybody ID it, get a plate?"

"A witness, a pizza delivery guy, saw the whole thing," Warren said. "We have a description of the vehicle, including license, but unfortunately the car was just found in the Bronx. Looks like they switched vehicles."

Yeah, and they've probably switched vehicles two more times already, Scott thought.

Scott knew how Willie Dugan worked, and this situation was pure Willie Dugan. This was a man who had spent nine years building a tunnel to escape from Attica. He always worked out his plans to the very last detail. But what did Cassie get him? It wasn't like Dugan to go after a man's daughter when he could go after the man himself. If he was willing to gun down a federal officer, why hadn't he just sent guys to shoot Scott and Carlos? Why bother with Cassie at all?

"How could you let this happen?" Scott said. "You had one job—to protect her."

"And we did our best," Warren yelled back. "We're still doing our best. When people start shooting, there's a limit to what we can do—whether we're trying to protect your daughter or the president of the United States. But we're doing everything we possibly can, using all available resources, to find your daughter. That's our number-one priority."

Scott was still furious at Warren, but he didn't want to get into a blaming match right now. He needed Warren to be 100-percent focused on finding Cassie. Besides, Scott knew he wasn't being entirely fair: He was the one who'd dismissed the threats from Dugan, who hadn't believed Dugan would target him or his family.

"All right," Scott said, "let's just find her."

Another agent came over and led Warren away. Scott spotted Carlos at the other end of the block, obviously looking around for him. Scott moved behind a parked SUV to avoid being seen as his phone rang. He grabbed it from his pocket during the first ring, praying it was Cassie, but it was Peggy.

Bracing himself, knowing hell itself was coming, Scott took the call and said, "You heard."

"Please..." She was crying. "Please tell me it isn't true."

"It is," Scott said, "but I'll find her. I—"

"This is your fault!" she screamed. "Your fault!"

He'd only heard that a few hundred thousand times during his marriage.

"Look, this isn't the time to blame—"

"Ant-Man," she said. "Stupid Ant-Man and all your stupid secrets."

"This has nothing to do with any of that," Scott said, realizing this was a ridiculous statement. Then he added, "Are you alone right now?"

"See?" she said. "All you care about is your stupid secret—that's all you ever care about."

"Peggy, please, try to—"

"Calm down?" Peggy said. "You're going to tell me to calm down? I knew I was making a mistake when I left Cassie with you. An ex-con! But I didn't think you'd mess up this bad, Scott, I didn't think you'd let anything...what's this all about, anyway? I need to know."

"Look, this isn't the time—"

"I just want my baby back." She was crying. "I want my baby to be safe."

"Trust me..." Scott was getting emotional, too, felt warm tears sliding down his cheeks. He said, "I want the same thing you do. I promise you, I'll get her back, and I'll make whoever's responsible pay for this."

"I've had it with your promises," Peggy said. "I'm coming to New York."

"Don't," Scott said. "That's a mistake. There's nothing you can do for her here, and it's safer to stay put."

"I have to do something," she said. "My baby needs me."

Scott's phone vibrated—an incoming text.

It was from a strange, non-New York City area code: 859. Could it be from Cassie? Had she gotten to a phone somehow?

"I have to call you back," Scott said.

Peggy said, "Scott, don't—"

He ended the call and tapped the message. It read:

> If you want to see your daughter alive call back from
> a disposable phone in 5 minutes

Scott cursed loudly. A couple of cops nearby looked over at him. Then another message from the same number:

> NO COPS

Scott looked around frantically, wondering whether the person who'd sent the text was here, at the crime scene. Then Scott spotted Carlos passing through the crowd, searching for him. Scott needed to avoid Carlos. With the marshal around, it would be impossible to call the number in privacy.

Skirting the crowd and Carlos, Scott ducked into a drugstore a block away and got in line at the register where the pay-as-you-go phones were located. There were two people ahead of him—an older woman who was fishing in her purse for change to finish paying for her purchase, and a guy with long hair, glasses, and a backwards Brooklyn Dodgers cap.

Scott checked his phone—it had been three minutes since he'd gotten the text, so he had two minutes to buy the phone and call back.

The woman was saying, "I know I have another nickel in here somewhere."

"Please, I'm in a huge rush," Scott said.

"You're gonna have to wait," the clerk, a young guy, replied.

Again, Scott wished he were in his Ant-Man suit. While he hadn't stolen anything in years, there were situations when shoplifting was permissible, and one of those situations was when your daughter has been abducted and you have two more minutes to purchase a phone to call the kidnapper. He could've gone behind the counter, removed a phone from the display, and left the store—hoping nobody noticed the odd sight of a phone carried by an ant-sized man.

The woman said, "Looks like I'll have to break the dollar."

When she finally finished her purchase, the guy in the baseball cap, noticing Scott's agitation, said to him, "It's okay, man, you can go ahead of me. No worries."

Who said New Yorkers were unfriendly?

"I need one of those phones," Scott said to the cashier.

"Which one?" he asked.

"Any one," Scott said. "That one—right there."

The cashier had to get a key from the manager to open the display case and take out the phone. Scott paid for it with a credit card, and then rushed out of the store. He went around the corner to Seventy-Fifth Street and ducked into the vestibule entranceway of a building.

He had a minute—or less, if whoever had texted had started timing when the text had been sent, rather than when it was received. Sweaty and frantic, Scott activated the phone as fast as he could, then dialed the 859 number.

Someone picked up.

TWELVE

LONG time no hear," Willie Dugan said, "and just in the nick of time."

Scott hadn't heard Willie Dugan's voice for many years—Dugan had opted not to testify and didn't say a word in public during his murder trial. But there was no doubt it was him.

"I want to talk to her, right now," Scott said.

"That's rude," Dugan said. "Haven't spoken in years, and I get no chitchat? No what's up, how you been? Aren't you curious? Don't you care what I've been up to?"

"Put her on right now, Willie."

"Ooh, testy, aren't we? What, you got anger-management issues now, Scott? You used to be such a calm guy, listened to Bob Dylan and Cat Stevens. Played a little acoustic, too, if I remember correctly."

"Willie, just put her on the phone."

"I'm sorry, she's not available at the moment. Would you care to leave a message?" Willie laughed.

Scott had normal blood pressure, but now the top number had to be one-eighty or higher.

"I swear," Scott said, "if you hurt her, I will hunt you down and kill you."

"Say that with an Irish accent, and you'll sound just like Liam

Neeson." Dugan laughed again.

"I wasn't joking," Scott said.

"Oh, I didn't think you were," Dugan said. "So you're surprised I'm alive? I mean, everybody's been reporting me dead for days."

"I'm not surprised," Scott said.

"I don't believe that," Dugan said. "I know how you are—always Mr. Optimistic. Part of you wanted to believe I was dead, that this was all over, even if the smart part of you knew I wasn't."

"How did you do it?" Scott asked, figuring he had a better chance of finding out information from Dugan if he was conversational with him, kept him on the line.

"I'm kinda surprised they didn't figure it out by now," Dugan said. "I mean with all that fancy DNA equipment they have nowadays. I'm also surprised nobody reported Mulligan missing yet."

"Mulligan?" Scott asked.

"Lawrence Mulligan," Dugan said. "You remember, the judge who presided at the trial. You know, the one where you ratted on me."

Now Scott recalled the name.

"Wait," Scott said, "so you mean—"

"Yeah, I killed the bastard," Dugan said. "He retired down to New Orleans. Lived alone, I guess that's why nobody reported him missing yet. But I figured if I set it up to look like I was dead, it would give me a better chance of getting at you. Oh, and your little girl."

"You son of a bitch," Scott said. "If you hurt her, I'll kill you."

"Whoa, Scotty, this isn't like you at all." Dugan sounded like he was enjoying this conversation. "I mean, you're not some lowlife vigilante like that guy Castle. Ant-Man doesn't kill people—he brings them to justice, right?"

How had Dugan found out Scott was Ant-Man? Had Cassie told him? Scott didn't think she would—unless she were threatened or tortured.

"I have no idea what you're talking about," Scott said.

"You can play dumb all you want," Dugan said, "but I know the truth. Figured it out a while ago, while I was in prison. I knew you knew Hank Pym, that doctor—you told me all about him. Then there was the fire at that motel. How did I get out of that? It was a freaking miracle—or was it? The firefighters told me it looked like I jumped out of the window, but I knew I was trapped up there, too weak to even move. There was no way I got up, went to the window, and jumped. I mean, not all by myself. I was passing out, dying, until…well, you tell me the rest, Scott."

Scott didn't know why Dugan was going on about this, but he had to keep him on the line. He needed to find out where Cassie was, and make sure she was okay.

"I don't know what this has to do with Cassie," Scott said.

"You thought I was an idiot?" Dugan said. "You thought I wasn't going to figure it out?"

"If she's with you now, could you just—"

"I'm not talking about your stupid daughter!" Dugan yelled. Then Scott heard him take a few deep breaths, as if trying to calm himself.

Jesus, this guy sounded totally unhinged, and he had Cassie. This was the worst nightmare imaginable.

Dugan continued, "I mean, I admit it took me a while to put it all together. It was the timing that gave it away. You tell me you're leaving my crew, you want to go straight, and then I start hearing about Ant-Man in the news. He uses the Pym Particles in his belt or whatever, shrinks to the size of an ant, and works with all the big shots—Iron Man, Captain America, even Spider-Man—helping to rid the world of evil and all that crap. Lot of rumors going around, too. Everybody's wondering, Who is this shrinking guy? Is he my friend? My neighbor? Did Hank Pym pass on the Ant-Man tech to somebody else?

"Then I get busted, my trial comes up, and who do they put on the stand to testify against me? My former loyal partner. That fits in, too—it was another piece of the puzzle. That's why you testified against me, huh? 'Cause you became so self-righteous? So this big change of heart you had led to me going away, a life sentence, and meanwhile you get to live this fancy life in the big city, pretending you're a hero. Yeah, I used the word 'pretending' 'cause that's what it is. It's all fake, an act.

"You know I thought about you every day in prison? I thought about what I'd do to get even with you. I had some other people on my list, but I was just warming up with them—you're my big prize, Scott. Every day when I was building that tunnel with my hands—yeah, that's right, my *hands*—I was thinking about you, how you betrayed me. And with every fistful of dirt, I was getting closer to the day I'd get even with you. Maybe you can fool them, Scott, but you can't fool me. I know who you are. I know *what* you are. Just 'cause you have some fancy suit doesn't make you into somebody you're not. You're no hero, Scott."

Scott didn't feel any remorse; he knew he'd done the right thing. But he had to try to calm Dugan down, try to reason with the lunatic.

"Why would you want to hurt me or my daughter?" Scott asked. "I mean, I get that you're upset about me testifying, but if what you're saying is true—and I'm not saying it is—then I saved your life."

"Life?" Dugan said, sounding shocked. "I didn't get to live life, I got to *do* life. You were away that time for, what, six months? A year?"

"Almost two years," Scott said.

"Two years at some country club compared to what I went through in max at Attica. You know what kind of animals I was in with? You know what hell I went through? And you call that a life?"

"I know you've been through hell," Scott said, "and I'm sorry things went down the way they did. But we're talking about my daughter, man. She has nothing to do with this. You have a problem with me, come after me. Fight me like a man."

Dugan was laughing.

"What?" Scott said. "What's funny? I'm being serious. Let her go, and I'll meet you anywhere you want."

Still laughing, Dugan said, "Man, you haven't changed, have you? Always thought you were the smartest one in the room. Well, guess what? You're not."

"That's right, 'cause *you're* the smart guy," Scott said. "You know how to make good decisions, I know you do. I remember how you used to plot out those jobs, right down to the last detail. You knew when you were outnumbered, outgunned, and you never made a wrong move. You can make the right decision now, Willie. You can—"

"Stop talking—you're making my head hurt," Dugan said. "I'm never going back inside, don't you get it? When I went into that tunnel, I knew that was it—there was no turning back. I had to get to the end of it, or I was gonna die trying—those were the only two options. But I didn't die, I got out, and now it's my time. Now it's time for some payback."

Scott was having trouble following Dugan, but he said, "I get what you're saying. You're frustrated, you're angry. Anybody would be in your situation, but that doesn't mean you have to—"

"I'm gonna text an address to this number after I hang up," Dugan said. "Come tonight, six o'clock, alone. I see a cop, or I think I see a cop, I'm gonna put one in your daughter's head."

Scott's face was hot with rage, but he maintained enough composure to say, "I'll be there."

The call ended.

Scott remained in the vestibule, waiting for the text to arrive. All he could think about was Dugan's threat to kill Cassie. It was hard for Scott to believe that he'd once spent so much time with this psycho, that he'd actually liked him. At the trial Scott had seen a different Willie Dugan, heard about the horrible things he'd done, how he'd become callous and hateful. If Dugan still had any remaining morality at that point, prison had wiped it away. Now he was full-blown deranged, deluded beyond repair. Had Dugan been hiding his true self from Scott all along? Or had the signs always been there, but Scott—wrapped up in his own problems—had chosen to ignore them?

The text arrived—an address in Wallkill, New York. Wallkill? Wasn't there a prison there? Scott Googled it—yep, the Wallkill Correctional Facility. That made sense, actually—well, it did if you were Willie Dugan. Willie used to say that the best place to hide out from the cops was right next door to a police station because it's the last place the cops would expect to find you. Taking that a step further: If you were an escaped convict, one of the most wanted men in America, where was the safest place to hide? How about in a town where there was *another* prison?

While Scott was on Google, he mapped Wallkill—it was upstate, in the Catskills, about an hour and a half from the city. It was four o'clock now. How did Dugan expect Scott to get up there so fast?

Scott texted:

I need more time

Got back:

6 or she gets a bullet and don't text here again, phone about to be destroyed

Scott cursed, then headed toward Second Avenue. He figured he'd take a roundabout route back to his apartment, going a block out of the way, to avoid running into Carlos.

Then, from behind him, Scott heard, "Hey, where you going?"

Scott stopped, turned back.

"I've been looking all over for you," Carlos said. "You can't be alone right now—it's way too dangerous."

"Sorry. I, uh, just had to get away for a little while."

Scott was still holding the pay-as-you-go phone. He slipped it into his pocket.

"Where you headed now?" Carlos asked.

"I was just going to head home," Scott said. "Wait for news there."

"You're heading in the wrong direction."

"Oh yeah," Scott said, pretending to be disoriented. "You're right."

"I'll walk you back," Carlos said. "I gotta make sure your place is secure, and I want to stay with you, too. I can't imagine what's going on in your head right now."

What was going on in Scott's head: planning how fast he could ditch Carlos and get his ass to Wallkill.

At the building, Carlos came up to Scott's apartment, looked around, then said, "I can hang out with you here if you want?"

"No, it's okay. I have things I need to do right now."

His cell, his *real* cell, rang. Scott checked the display and saw: Tony Stark.

"Gotta take this—it's my ex-wife," Scott lied.

"I'll be downstairs if you need me," Carlos said.

When Carlos was gone, Scott answered the call.

"Just heard what happened," Tony said. "Let's go—I'll help you find Cassie."

It would have been nice to fly to Wallkill at jet speed. But remembering Dugan's warning to show up alone, Scott said, "It's okay, Tone, I got this."

"You sure?" Stark said. "We're talking about your daughter. This is no time to be proud, man."

Scott wasn't making the decision out of pride. If he'd thought Tony coming along would increase his chances of bringing Cassie home safely, of course he'd accept the help.

"No, it's all right," Scott said. "Seriously, I appreciate it. If I need backup I'll give you a shout, but I don't think that will be the case."

"So you know where this guy is?" Tony asked.

Scott didn't answer.

"I'll take that as a yes. Okay, Scott, this is your call, obviously. I'm sure you have it under control, but be careful. This Willie Dugan guy sounds like he has nothing to lose, which is the most dangerous kind of criminal."

Scott was crouching in the closet, dialing in the combination to the safe.

"Don't worry." He opened the safe, revealing the Ant-Man suit. "I'm bringing my A-game."

AS SCOTT put on the suit, he felt his pulse pounding as usual. This was what he was meant to do with his life—it was his calling; it felt right. As a man, he was just another working guy, an anonymous face in the crowd. But when he put on the suit—gaining strength as he shrunk—he became a fighter, a leader. It was why Hank Pym had entrusted him with the power. Some people were meant to be doctors, or teachers, or construction workers, or presidents. Scott was meant to be Ant-Man.

The helmet came out of the suit, and Scott clicked it into place. He released the gas with the Pym Particles—and then boom, he shrunk. What a rush! He'd transformed hundreds, maybe thousands, of times over the years, but he'd never stop feeling awed by the technology, his suddenly fresh perspective on the world. Becoming tiny never made him feel insignificant—it made him feel huge.

But the feeling of greatness wasn't just physical—it was psychological. As a man, Scott's senses were limited to his thoughts and feelings—but as Ant-Man, he had a larger awareness and natural understanding of how the universe worked. Being ant-sized showed him how limited the human perspective was—there was a bigger world around us that we simply couldn't understand. Maybe the technology brought him closer to what the Buddhists sought: pure consciousness. On some super-subconscious level, he was aware of all the ants in the building, another world of friends ready to support him like loyal soldiers. Scott didn't fully trust humans—most people had disappointed him or turned on him at some point—but he'd never met an ant he didn't like.

The euphoria was fleeting, though, overtaken by his only concern: finding Cassie and bringing her home to safety.

Scott skidded out of the apartment and leaped down the stairs one floor at a time. He knew he could be heading toward some kind of trap. Dugan always had a plan, a method to his madness—and this time the plan was probably related to Scott's identity as Ant-Man. That's why Dugan had kidnapped Cassie rather than Scott—because he knew that Scott would come to Wallkill as Ant-Man. But Scott had no idea what the rest of Dugan's plan entailed. Maybe he was going to try to convince Scott to use his powers as Ant-Man to pull off some crime, to rob a bank or a Brink's truck. Or maybe Dugan's plan was to lure Scott upstate simply to kill him—and Cassie, too.

Outside the apartment building, Carlos was on his cell, probably talking to some FBI colleague. "...Yes, he's inside now...Yes, I'll do that...Yes, okay, got you, no problem...Yes..."

Scott zipped by him, unseen. He knew Carlos would catch some serious flack for letting Scott disappear under his watch, especially since it had just happened the other day when Roger had let Cassie slip away. But that was the least of Scott's concerns.

He sprinted along the sidewalk, faster than he could ever move at his normal size. At the corner, he leapt onto the top of a taxi heading uptown and clung to the roof.

It was probably about 4:15 now, so he had to beat rush hour out of the city if he had any chance of getting to Wallkill by the six o'clock deadline.

Finally, he felt like himself—his true self. He was sick of playing the victim, hiding under a Protection Order, taking all the punches.

It was time for Ant-Man.

It was time to fight back.

THIRTEEN

CASSIE was in the dark and couldn't make a sound.

While she was passed out, the men had covered her eyes with a blindfold, or tape, or maybe both, and taped her mouth, too, so she couldn't scream. Then they'd dragged her out of the car and into other cars a few times. They kept telling her to stay calm and do what they said and everything would fine. She didn't believe them, but she also knew that her dad was going to come and save her. Maybe he'd come alone, or maybe Iron Man or Spider-Man would come, too, and rescue her, bring these guys to justice.

But now she wasn't so sure.

She had no idea where she was or how her dad could possibly find her. She thought a couple of hours had gone by since she'd been kidnapped, but she was so scared, it was hard to keep track of time. And even if two hours had gone by, that didn't necessarily mean she was two hours outside of Manhattan. She'd read a Sherlock Holmes story for her English class last year where criminals kidnapped this guy and put him in the trunk of the car and took him someplace that seemed far away because a lot of time had gone by, but it turned out that was a trick. The criminals had been driving in circles the whole time. Cassie didn't think this had happened to her because she definitely wasn't in Manhattan. They'd taken her out of the car again, and the big guy kept telling her to "Stop crying" and "Just relax, honey." She could smell grass and flowers and fresh, clean country air.

She stopped walking and dragged her feet, refusing to go any farther.

"Come on," the big guy said. "You could make it hard, or you could make it easy."

She listened to his voice closely, knowing that if she got out of here alive, she might have to remember it. His voice was deep, and he had an accent. Boston? Long Island? She'd never been great with accents, that was the problem. Didn't they say "yahd" instead of "yard" in Boston? She'd keep listening, waiting for him to say yahd, then she'd know for sure. She knew she was being ridiculous, thinking about accents when her life was probably in danger, but she was too frightened to think about what was actually happening. She needed to think about something else, distract herself.

"Okay, looks like she wants it the hard way," the big guy said.

They each grabbed one of her arms and dragged her up the stairs into some building. It was a house—definitely a house. It smelled musty, but she also thought she smelled food—something spicy, maybe Mexican. She'd remember that, too, if someone asked her later. She had to be a detective, like Sherlock Holmes, and keep collecting all of the clues. That's how she'd think of this—like a game, a mystery.

A door creaked open. Doors creaked in old houses, right? So she was in an old house in the country where maybe Mexican people from Boston lived. Okay, it wasn't a lot, but it was still something.

The big guy told her to sit, so she sat in a chair—a wooden chair.

"If you promise not to yell or do anything stupid, I'll take the tape off your mouth. You think you can do that?"

Cassie didn't think he was from Boston anymore, but she didn't know where he was from. She nodded.

He said, "This might hurt," and he tore the tape off her mouth.

"Ow," she said.

"Remember," he said, "we're not messing around, so don't try anything stupid or the tape goes back on."

"Why're you doing this?" Cassie asked.

"Hey," the man said, "did I say you can ask questions?"

"I have to go to the bathroom," Cassie said.

"I think you're just saying that," the guy said.

"Why would I just say that?"

"Let her go to the bathroom," the shorter guy said.

Cassie liked the shorter guy better. He sounded nicer.

"Okay," the big guy said to Cassie, "but you better not try anything."

The big guy led her out of the room into the hallway. It still smelled like Mexican food, but it didn't make Cassie hungry—she was way too scared to be hungry.

"Okay, the bathroom's right here, go in," he said to her.

"How'm I going to go to the bathroom blindfolded?"

"It's right there on the left—feel around, you'll find it. And don't even think of trying to get out the window. It's bolted shut."

Cassie went into the bathroom and shut the door. She had a feeling he was lying about the last part, but she wasn't going to try anything stupid and get herself killed. She had to hope her dad could somehow save her. It was the best chance she had—maybe the only chance.

It was so gross, sitting on a toilet blindfolded. What if it was dirty like the toilet seats at school? But when you're worried about getting killed, a gross toilet seat doesn't seem to matter so much.

She thought about taking the blindfold off and at least looking out the window to see where she was, but she was afraid she wouldn't be able to get it back on. Besides, the big guy was right outside and might come in if he heard her walking toward the window.

She had to feel around to find the flusher and the sink. She'd never really thought about what blind people went through every day. If she got out of here alive, she was going to have more of an appreciation for what people with disabilities had to deal with on a daily basis. She would help whenever she could—doing community service, free tutoring, and anything else. She'd be a better person.

They brought her back to the same room. The big guy told her to sit in the chair, and then the other guy tied her up with rope.

"How long are you planning to keep me here?" she asked.

"That's up to your father," the big guy said.

"What do you want from him?" Cassie asked. "He wasn't bothering you; he wasn't bothering anybody." Then Cassie looked toward where she thought the shorter guy was standing and said, "Why are you doing this to me? Can't you tell him to let me go? Please, I won't tell anyone what happened. Just drop me back in Manhattan, and I'll make up a story that I ran away or that I was hiding. Actually that's what I told people the other day, that I was hiding, when I was really…" In her nervousness she almost blurted out that she had put on her dad's Ant-Man suit. Instead, she continued, "Anyway, people will believe it, and I won't tell them anything about you guys. I won't tell them that the house smells like Mexican food. I'm great at keeping secrets. Seriously, it's one of my greatest talents."

"Hey, do yourself a favor and keep your mouth shut, will ya?" the big guy said.

She continued to the shorter guy, "Please. I know you're not like your friend. I can tell you're a good person—you're different."

She hoped he *was* different, that he would turn on the big guy, maybe get out his gun or something.

But it turned out he wasn't different, after all, or else he was just a big wimp, because when they finished tying her up, he and the big guy left the room without another word.

Cassie was trying to be a big girl. She knew crying wouldn't get her father here any quicker.

But she also knew that being so calm in this situation wasn't normal. She was probably in shock, and had been in shock since the big guy had shot Roger and the guys forced her into the car.

Roger had been shot, actually shot.

Thinking about it now, it seemed surreal, like a nightmare. Cassie hoped he was okay. He had probably been wearing a bullet-proof vest, so maybe he was alive—unless the man had shot him in the face. Why would these men shoot a federal marshal just to kid-nap her? It had to do with her dad and Ant-Man, obviously. As usual, her dad's big secrets had caused chaos in her life. All the moving around they'd done when she was a kid, the whole divorce thing with her mom—it was all because of her dad and Ant-Man. And now, if she got killed, it was going to be his fault, too.

She was so angry at him, but she also needed him to come save her. She didn't know how she was supposed to feel about her father, whether she should hate him or love him. It was the story of her life.

Now she couldn't stop herself from crying—she felt too scared, too alone. Why did life have to be so cruel, so unfair? This had gone from the best day of her life to the worst day, in a split second. She'd been so happy at school after finding out that Tucker liked her. She'd imagined kissing Tucker so many times, how his lips and tongue would feel. She'd never kissed anyone before, actually. What if she died without kissing anyone? It was so unfair—she hadn't done anything to deserve this. Or had she? Maybe it was, like, karma. Because she'd broken Nikki's nose with the basketball, she'd been kidnapped and might never have a chance to kiss Tucker.

She heard footsteps coming from the hallway, and then the door opened and someone entered the room. It was a man—she could tell by the body odor. It was really bad.

"So you're Scott Lang's daughter, huh?" the man said.

His voice sounded gravelly, like a smoker's. His age? Maybe fifties or sixties, definitely older than her dad. There was something creepy about him, too. Not just the way he spoke—his whole vibe.

"I remember when you were born," he said. "Used to sit on my lap. I knew you'd grow up pretty someday."

Definitely creepy.

"Who are you?" Cassie asked. "What do you want?"

"Yeah, your father's daughter, all right. Feisty little thing, aren't you? That's the thing I admired most about your dad. He was a fighter, not a whiner. He never gave up."

"You better not hurt me," Cassie said. "And you better let me go, or I'm telling you right now, my dad will track you down, he'll find you and—"

"Don't worry, your father's already on his way up here."

"He is?" Cassie wondered whether he was lying.

"Yeah," the man said. "Spoke to him on the phone before, and he should be here by six o'clock."

Still thinking this was some kind of trick, Cassie asked, "If that's true, then why are you so relaxed?"

"What do you mean?" the man said. "Is there a reason I should be afraid of your father? I mean, if he's really just some regular working guy in Manhattan, what can he do to hurt me?"

Cassie could tell the man was hinting about her dad's identity as Ant-Man. But he didn't sound like he knew for sure that her dad was Ant-Man, either.

"He's my dad," she said. "Dads get angry when their daughters are in danger."

"Oh wow, I don't want an angry dad coming after me," the man said.

"You're being sarcastic," Cassie said.

"Okay, you want serious, I'll give you serious," the man said.

This was it—he was going to shoot her. Cassie thought about Tucker, his lips, kissing them. This was the last thought she wanted to have.

But the man didn't shoot her. She was still breathing, still thinking about Tucker's lips.

The man said, "I was a friend of your dad's. We used to work together. This was a long time ago—like ten, fifteen years ago."

Cassie's pulse was still pounding—either from nearly dying or from nearly fantasy-kissing Tucker, she couldn't tell which.

"I get it," Cassie said. "You're a criminal, just like my dad was."

"Criminal's a harsh word," the man said, "but, yeah, we lived the life together. I trusted your father, literally trusted him with my life, but then he did something bad—something to betray me."

Cassie said, "You're the one who's after my dad, right? You're why we've had to be protected."

"No, I'm not after him," the man said. "I just want to make a deal with him, that's all. If he cooperates, I'll let you go. It's all up to him."

"My dad's not a bad person," Cassie said. "He wouldn't do something bad to you unless you deserved it."

Just like I deserve to be here for what I did to Nikki, Cassie thought.

"Yeah, well, maybe you're a smart kid, but you don't know everything," the man said. "Your dad did the worst thing a man can do to another man—he testified against me. You know what that means?"

"I'm fourteen, not four. Of course I know what that means."

Snapping at the man made her felt stronger, more powerful. She managed to forget for a few seconds that she was tied to a chair and blindfolded, and had no power at all.

"Criminals like us—I mean real criminals, pros—we all take an oath," the man said. "Not the kind of oath you take in a courtroom, not an oath to God. An oath just for us. Trust. I'm talking about trust. I trusted your father never to turn on me, and that's exactly what he did. Worse, he did it to save his own ass. Putting yourself before your friend? What kind of man does that? And because of what he did to me, how he turned on me, I spent nine years in hell. Nine years of my life living in a cage, like an animal. But now I'm out of my cage—and I'll tell you right now, I'm never going back in there again."

One of Cassie's greatest skills in life was her ability to spot crazy people. Sometimes in the city she'd be hanging out with her friends at a Starbucks or wherever, and she'd go to one of her friends, "Hey, look at that guy over there—he's crazy," and her friends would be like, "What do you mean? What guy?" And then the guy would do something totally crazy—like yell in somebody's face, or start a fight—and Cassie would say to her friends, "See?" She was always right. And now her "crazydar" was, well, going crazy, telling her that this man was crazy. He had probably killed people before, and could easily kill again.

"If my dad testified against you, he must've had a good reason," Cassie said.

She didn't know where she was getting all this courage to stand up to the man, to say how she felt, but she wasn't afraid anymore at all.

"He had no reason!" the man screamed, so loud it hurt Cassie's ears. "No reason!"

Her crazydar was right again.

Cassie thought the man might hit her or something. She braced herself, but he said, "I have some information aboutyour dad, and I've been trying to figure out if it's true or not. If you help me out, there may be a, well, better outcome for you and your dad. It's up to you."

Again, Cassie thought he was hinting about Ant-Man, though she didn't know for sure. But one thing she did know: He wasn't going to just let her go, no matter what she told him. She'd seen those guys shoot Roger, so why wouldn't they shoot her, too? If her dad didn't show up to save her, she was definitely going to die. So there was no way she was telling the man anything.

"What kind of information?" she asked.

"I think you know what I'm talking about," he said.

"No, I don't know."

He let out a deep breath, then said, "You and your dad sound like you're pretty close, huh?"

"Yeah," she said. "So?"

"Did he ever talk about his secret life?"

Yeah, this was about Ant-Man. Wow, it was amazing how right she always was about people. Maybe when she grew up she should become a psychologist? Well, *if* she grew up—and right now, that was a very big if.

"No," Cassie said. "Never."

"You ever notice that there's something different about your dad?" he asked. "I mean, as far as how he can talk to insects."

"Insects?"

"Yeah," the man said. "Or really I mean ants."

"*Ants?*" Cassie said. "I have no idea what you're talking about."

"Fine, I'll just come out and ask it," the man said. "Your dad's Ant-Man, right?"

"What? What're you talking about?

"He knows Pym, this scientist," the man said. "Pym gave him a suit."

"I have no idea what you're talking about," Cassie said. "My dad's just my dad. Wait, is that what this is all about? That's why you're doing this to me, because you really think...oh my god, this is so crazy. I can't believe this is happening."

Hey, her acting wasn't too bad. If she did make it out of here, she would seriously consider auditioning for one of the school plays next year.

"I think you're lying," the man said.

Well, maybe her acting wasn't *that* good.

She kept trying, though. "Think about it," she said. "If my dad was Ant-Man, why would the FBI be protecting us from you? Did you ever think about that? If he was a super hero, he wouldn't need any protection. He'd be able to protect himself, right?"

It was quiet. Cassie was proud of herself for coming up with that stuff about the FBI. It seemed to have had an effect on the guy—got him thinking, anyway.

Then he said, "You're his daughter, all right. You're stubborn, just like Scott. But you know what? I believe in hunches, and I got a hunch you're holding back on me. Lemme tell you, you're making a big mistake—a mistake that might cost you your life."

"Oh, stop trying to scare me, already," Cassie said. "It's getting old. I'm not scared of you—I'm not scared of anything—so it's not going to work."

"Yeah," he said, "just like your dad."

Then she heard him walk out of the room, and the door slammed shut.

Cassie had no idea what to expect next. She wasn't sure what time it was—day or night. She thought it was still day, because she wasn't too tired or hungry. But what would happen later? Would they feed her? Where would she sleep?

In the movies, when people were tied to a chair, they just jiggled their hands a little, and in a few seconds that was it—they were free. But in real life, it was much more difficult—maybe impossible. Cassie tried to move her arms around to see whether the ropes would loosen, but the men had tied her too tightly. She kept trying; finally, the ropes around one of her hands loosened a little.

Then she heard the gunshots.

She tried telling herself that they'd come from a TV, that they weren't real, but she couldn't fool herself. There had been four shots, maybe five, and she heard a man screaming, or maybe wailing—it was all happening too far away to tell. And then there was another shot, and everything got quiet.

The quiet was the scariest part. She wanted to scream, but she was too afraid. With the blindfold still on securely, she couldn't see anything—which somehow made the quiet seem quieter. Then she had a horrifying thought: What if everybody in the house was dead? And what if her father never came? She could stay tied up here in the chair for days, until she eventually died.

She kept squirming, pulling at the ropes.

For a long time—or maybe it just seemed like a long time—there was total silence. Then there were steps. Someone was coming down the hallway, toward the room, and then the door creaked open.

If this was it, if she was going to die, she wanted it to happen fast. At least that would be better than having to stay tied to the chair and starving to death. In a few seconds, it would be over. She'd stop thinking, and she'd never be scared again. She hated being scared.

Cassie heard a click. She'd never fired a gun before, but she'd seen a lot of TV shows and movies with guns, and she knew what the click of a gun sounded like.

"Go ahead," she said. "Just do it. I don't care."

Maybe she was in shock, because she wasn't really feeling anything. Well, nothing except numbness. There was nothing she could do to stop it, nothing at all. She'd never have her first kiss, never see Tucker's face again. Everything was dark, and she would stay in the darkness forever.

But the shot didn't come. Cassie heard footsteps leave the room and fade down the hallway. She was alone again.

FOURTEEN

JUMPING from car to car, Scott made his way across the GW Bridge and onto the Palisades Parkway. He was able to check the route and time with the helmet's newest technology, which sort of worked like Tony Stark's HUD, with voice-activation and images appearing in front of his eyes. Scott had sort of, well, *borrowed* the tech from Tony. Tony was cool with it, though: Scott and Tony were always competing with each other and riffing off each other's latest inventions. Since Scott had moved to New York, he hadn't had as much free time to tinker with the tech, but he was always coming up with improvements. Working on the Ant-Man suit was an absorbing, endless project.

Scott was making good time; he was easily on target to reach Wallkill by the 6 p.m. deadline. He had to make it on time, and Cassie *had* to be okay. Any other possibility was off the table. It wouldn't get dark until 7:30 or 8—and even that didn't matter, because he had night vision. The only thing that could slow him down was traffic, and that's exactly what he hit approaching the exit for I-87.

The traffic was bumper-to-bumper. Scott managed to jump from car to car and make some progress. He could move quickly as Ant-Man, but not at fifty-five miles per hour. He jumped onto the back of a motorcyclist who was driving along the shoulder to beat the traffic, but even that only speeded him up a little bit.

Finally, he latched onto the roof of a bus and made it to the exit. The cars were moving well on 87, but the traffic had cost him a good twenty minutes. A map flashed in front of him: GPS estimated that he would now arrive at the location in Wallkill at 5:44. That didn't give him much wiggle room to make the 6 o'clock deadline.

Scott hopped another bus onto I-84. When the bus exited, he tried to jump on top of a car, but—maybe because he was so concerned with the time—he misjudged the leap and landed on the edge of the car's trunk. He tried to grab on, but he lost his grip and fell onto the highway. A few cars passed right over him, the wheels barely missing him. He got back on his feet and jumped cleanly onto the roof of a car in the next lane, and was back on his way.

The fall had cost him a little time, but not much. He exited in Newburgh and managed to make it most of the way to Wallkill on the back of a pickup truck. He had to jump off about a quarter of a mile away from the address when the pickup headed in the wrong direction, and then he jumped onto the fender of another truck to make it the rest of the way.

He arrived at 5:47, ahead of the deadline. From his ant POV, he zoomed in on the house. It definitely didn't seem like someplace where a wanted criminal would be living, but that was the whole point—if Dugan wanted to blend in, go unnoticed as a felon, he'd picked the perfect spot. Not only was it near a high-security prison—only a half mile away, according Scott's GPS—but it was an ordinary, working-class Upstate New York country house, complete with an American flag hanging from a pole on the front porch.

While Scott had arrived in Wallkill unnoticed by humans, his presence had piqued the curiosity of the local ant community. There were many more ants up here, obviously, than in Manhattan. Thousands of them came out from their nests and hills to witness Scott's arrival. Aided by what Scott thought of as his ant telepathy, he knew that the ants were excited and curious to see him. He sent a telepathic message back to them that he had great respect for them, and that he was here because his daughter was in danger.

An elder ant, a leader of a local colony, came forward. Scott sensed the support of the ants.

Scott responded with a message that conveyed the sentiment: *Thank you. It gives me strength knowing you are here supporting me.*

Sometimes Scott's abilities as Ant-Man seemed like second nature to him; at other times, like right now, the whole thing seemed utterly absurd. While geeking out with the suit was always a blast, sometimes he didn't know whether being Ant-Man was worth the price.

He had promised Hank Pym that he would use his powers for good rather than evil, and he'd saved many lives, but there were consequences. While helping others, he'd hurt his own family—the stress of his responsibilities and maintaining his secret identity had definitely been factors in his divorce—and now, worst of all, he'd put his daughter in danger. At times like this, it was hard not to hate what he'd become.

Then Scott heard the shots—one, then several more in quick succession, coming from inside the house. As he sped under the door, his worries about Willie Dugan's hidden agenda vanished. His only concern was finding his daughter.

He was in what seemed to be the living room. When he looked into the adjacent dining room, he could see a man's legs on the ground. As he got closer, he saw the puddle of blood; not wanting to get drenched in it, he leapt onto the dining table to get a better view of the room. Lying near the door was Ricky Gagliardi, the guy Scott had known. There were two other bodies at the other end of the room—two other men who'd been shot. One he didn't recognize, but the other he would never have trouble ID'ing—even on his side, with a bullet hole in his head.

Willie Dugan.

"Cassie!" Scott called out. "Cassie!"

Even at tiny size, in his Ant-Man suit, he could project his voice to its normal human volume.

He leapt off the table, skirted around Dugan's body, and sprinted up the hallway. He heard movement upstairs—footsteps, a creak in the old floorboards. Was Cassie up there, or the killer?

He was about to go up to check when he spotted a door at the far end of the hallway. He zoomed in and saw that it had a bolt on the *outside.* Why was it bolted, unless there was someone in there?

But Scott had a great backup plan. The local ants had followed Scott into the house, and he told them to spread the word to all ants in the area: Barricade the house. The ants rushed away to relay the message. Scott didn't think there was time for the ants to assemble in a mass large enough to actually help him, but it was worth a shot.

Meanwhile, Scott went under the door into the locked room. Sure enough, there was Cassie. She was in the middle of the room, bound and blindfolded, tied to a chair. She was wriggling her hands, trying to get free.

"Cass, baby, are you okay?"

"Daddy, is...is that you?"

She sounded fine, but he hoped to God she hadn't been hurt in any way. Willie Dugan was lucky he was dead, or Scott would have beaten the living crap out of him.

"Yeah, it's me. Did they hurt you?"

"No, nobody hurt me. I can't believe you're really here, Daddy. I love you so much."

"I love you too, Bear."

Scott used to call Cassie "Bear" when she was a toddler, when she and Peggy had visited him in prison.

Scott jumped up onto Cassie's lap, then crawled onto her chin. She shook her head, trying to shake him away as if he were, well, a bug.

"It's me, Cassie, I'm on your chin now."

"I love you, Daddy," she said.

"I love you, too," Scott said, "more than anything."

He climbed along the rope holding Cassie to the chair and easily untied the knots, freeing her.

"How did you do that so fast?" she asked.

"Hold on," he said.

He latched onto the edge of the blindfold. It was held down with masking tape.

"This might hurt like a Band-Aid," he said. "Ready? One, two—" He leapt off her chin, clinging to the tape, and ripped it right off.

"Oww!" she screeched. Then said, "You never said three... Daddy? Where are you? *Daddy?*"

"Right here, Cass."

"Where?"

He waved to her from the floor, where he was unsticking himself from the seemingly gigantic piece of tape.

She saw the tape moving and said, "Oh my god, that is so freaky."

Scott discarded the tape, then said, "Okay, stand back."

He worked the suit's controls and his body reverted to its normal size.

"Holy..." Cassie was stunned, but also excited. "You are totally letting me do that again."

"When you're—"

"I know—twenty-one," Cassie said.

"Come here," Scott said.

He hugged her. He never wanted to let go.

"This was the scariest day of my life," he said. "We're never going through this again."

"Deal," Cassie said. Then she whispered, "I think someone else is in the house."

"I know," Scott said.

"I think I heard a gun click," Cassie whispered. "Somebody was going to shoot me when you got here."

Wow—had it really been that close? If he'd gotten here a little later, *on time*, would Cassie be dead now? Like Dugan and his friends?

"Keep your voice down," Scott said. "Get in the closet. I'll come right back for you."

"No, take me with you," Cassie whispered.

"Everything will be fine, I promise."

Scott kissed her on top of her head to assure her, the way he used to when she came to visit him in prison and he'd tell her, 'Everything'll be fine, sweet Bear, I promise. Daddy will be home soon.'

Cassie whispered, "Be careful, Daddy," and slipped into the closet.

Scott released the gas again and shrunk back to ant size. Then he left the room and stopped in the hallway, listening closely and surveying the scene. Everything looked the same, and he didn't hear any sounds upstairs. He did sense the presence of ants—lots of ants—outside the house and in the surrounding area.

He checked the hallway. Empty. He was about to leap up the stairs when he heard movement behind him. Was it an animal or a person? In the next instant, he was flat on his back, like an insect that had been sprayed with bug repellent. But unlike an insect, Scott couldn't even flail his legs. He couldn't move at all.

He had no idea what was going on. His body felt fine—he was breathing normally, didn't feel sick or hurt, and he could think normally—but he couldn't move. Then he heard an odd buzzing coming from the helmet, and when he tried to activate the HUD, the system had been disabled. He tried an override, but nothing happened.

He knew all of this was intentional; someone had done this to him for a reason.

Then he heard a car start.

"Cassie! Cassie, are you okay? Cass! Cass, answer me!"

Only a few minutes ago he'd promised that he'd never put her through anything bad again. Now he'd already reneged.

"Daddy?"

Thank god.

"Cass, I'm over here."

"Where?"

"Near the stairs."

"I don't see anything."

Her foot—the huge sneaker—came down right next to him with a loud, floor-shaking thud.

"Hey, careful," Scott said.

He didn't know whether this paralysis he was experiencing affected the suit's extra-cranial structure, and his overall strength, but he didn't want to take any chances. He wanted to expand back to human size, because he couldn't move his fingers to activate the Pym gas. He had a backup system, a way to activate the Pym gas via the HUD system, but that wouldn't work either, with his non-functioning helmet.

"There you are." Cassie crouched, her huge face looking down at Scott. "Why are you on your back like a dead bug?"

"Oh, I just thought it would be fun to do a little yoga, some back stretches," Scott said sarcastically. "Pick me up in your hand, quickly. And be careful—I don't know if there's anybody else in the house."

"I heard a car leave."

"I know, so did I," Scott said. "Come on, lift me."

"You mean you can't move?" Cassie asked.

"No," Scott said. "Now just do what I'm telling you to do."

Using her gigantic thumb and forefinger, Cassie lifted Scott off the ground.

"Now what?" she asked, and then accidentally let go of him. "Oh no!"

Scott fell to the floor; it seemed like he was jumping off a cliff. The impact shook him up a little, but didn't really hurt.

"Oh my god! Are you okay, Dad?" Cassie asked.

"Yes, but do what I tell you to do, okay? Put me in the palm of your hand and take me into the kitchen."

She did as she was told and said, "I guess the kitchen's this way," as she walked along the hallway.

"Don't look in the dining room," Scott instructed.

"Oh my God, I can see a guy's legs."

"I told you not to look."

"Is he dead?"

"Never mind that."

"I just want to get out of here and go home," Cassie said.

"Join the club," Scott said.

In the kitchen, Cassie asked, "What do you want me to do now?"

"Find a glass and fill it with water."

"What for?"

"Just do it."

Before she turned on the water, Scott screamed, "Wait!" He was afraid she might accidentally drop him down the drain. If he remained paralyzed, he'd have no chance to escape.

"What?" Cassie asked.

"Put me down on the floor, and then get the glass of water."

Cassie did it, then asked, "Now what?"

"Put the glass next to me on the floor, and then drop me in the water. This is important—as soon as you drop me, run out of the kitchen into the hallway. Run like a bomb's about to explode."

She lifted him up with her finger and held him over the glass. "You really want me to drop you in?" she asked. "You'll drown."

Scott couldn't rule out this possibility entirely, but he had to reassure his daughter.

He said, "Don't worry, I'll be fine—just remember to run for cover. Okay, on three. One, two—"

As Cassie let go, Scott was thinking, *You didn't let me get to three,* and then he splashed into the water—or at least, it felt like a splash. A human in the room would barely have seen a ripple.

He was hoping the water would jumpstart the flow of the Pym expanding gas. At first, nothing happened. Well, nothing except that he steadily sank toward the bottom of the glass. He was already struggling to breathe. Worse, he'd instructed Cassie to leave the room, so she couldn't save him. He tried to yell for her to help, but his voice was muffled by the water.

Then he saw tiny bubbles in the water, and an instant later *kaboom*—he returned to his human size in an explosion of glass.

Scott lay on his butt on the kitchen floor, stunned and dazed. He gasped a bit, thankful he could breathe at all. He could move, which was also good news.

"Cass?" he called out. "Cass, are you okay?"

Cassie came into the room, looked at Scott amid the glistening shards, and said, "What...what happened?"

Scott did a quick system eval—the Ant-Man helmet and HUD seemed totally back to normal now.

"I'll explain later," Scott said. "Come on, let's go."

He just wanted to get Cassie out of here, to safety. He'd unravel the mysteries later.

He opened the front door and looked in awe at the blackness.

"Wow," Cassie said. "Are those all *ants*?"

They were.

Tens of thousands of ants had swarmed the house. The ants closest to the door moved to either side, parting like the Red Sea—make that the Black Sea—to create space for Scott and Cassie to pass. Scott and Cassie continued toward the driveway, the ants in front of them providing a path.

There were two cars in the driveway. Scott could've gone back into the house and searched for car keys in the pockets of Willie Dugan or one of the other dead guys, but he had a quicker method.

He told Cassie to stand back, and then he activated the Pym gas. He shrunk to ant size, leapt up to the driver's side of the car and landed below the window, then crawled into the keyhole. He clicked open the lock; as he lunged backwards, the door swung open.

As Scott emerged from the car door, Cassie said, "You have to teach me how to do that someday."

"I'm not done," Scott said.

Inside the car, he crawled into the ignition and started the engine Then he emerged, exited the car, and returned to human size.

He'd accomplished all of this in less than twenty seconds.

"So awesome," Cassie said.

Scott always carried a set of spare clothes and a few hundred dollars in cash shrunken in a pouch attached to the suit. He put on the clothes—jeans, black T-shirt, black hoodie, and sneakers. The Ant-Man suit was awesome, but it felt great to be a normal human again after his near-death experience in the glass of water.

"Let's rock 'n' roll," he said.

Cassie got into the passenger seat, and they drove out of Wallkill and headed back to New York. During the car ride, Scott tried to reassure Cassie that she was safe now, that the men who'd abducted her were dead. Scott kept obsessing over the same question: Who was this behind this? This time Dugan was dead, and Scott didn't need a medical examiner to prove it. But who had killed Dugan and his crew, and was it the same person who'd zapped him?

"The guy who came into the room," Scott said to Cassie, "when you were tied up."

"What about him?" Cassie asked.

"Do you remember anything about him?"

"I was blindfolded."

"I know," Scott said. "But maybe there was something else. Did you hear something? Smell something?"

"No, but whoever it was, was bad," Cassie said. "I mean, I got a bad vibe." She sounded panicked. "Oh my god, what if he comes after me? What if I get kidnapped again?"

"Everything's going to be okay now," Scott said. "You're safe."

"You keep telling me that," Cassie said. "You told me the protection order would keep me safe, too, but it didn't. How do you know I'm safe now?"

"Hey, you've seen what Ant-Man can do," Scott said, trying to assure her. "You've worn the suit, experienced it yourself."

"Yeah, but it didn't do any good for you today," Cassie said.

"It got me upstate," Scott said. "It got me into the house."

"Yeah, and you also wound up on your back like a dying cockroach." Touché.

"I'm not sure how that happened," Scott said, "but I'm going to find out."

Scott tried to distract Cassie, talking about the future—positive things. He reminded her that soon she'd be back in school, with her friends, and then she had the whole summer to look forward to. She was going to sleepaway camp in the Poconos with Elly, an old friend of hers from San Francisco.

The distraction strategy worked for a few minutes, then Cassie got upset again and said, "I could've died in the chair, Daddy. If you hadn't shown up to save me, I'd be dead right now."

"And if you hadn't plopped me into that glass of water, you might've had a permanently paralyzed ant-sized dad," Scott said.

On the highway, they stopped at a rest area. Scott called Peggy on the phone he'd bought to call Dugan.

"Hello," she answered anxiously.

"Is a marshal with you?" Scott asked.

"Yes," Peggy said. "Why? What's going on? What happened?"

"Just wanted to let you know I have Cassie," Scott said. "She's safe."

"Oh, thank god. Can I speak to her?"

"Cassie, say hi to Mom."

Cassie leaned near the phone and said, "Hi, Mommy."

"Hi, Sweetie, I love you. Are you okay? Did they hurt you?"

"I'm totally fine," Cassie said. "Thanks to Daddy."

Scott was feeling emotional, but maintained his composure.

He said to Peggy, "This is important. Just tell the marshal we're on our way back to the city, and we're fine. We'll be back at our apartment soon."

"What do you mean?" Peggy asked. "Where are you?"

Scott knew they could trace the call, but it didn't matter. He and Cassie would be on the road again soon.

"We're safe, that's the important thing," Scott said. "Talk to you soon from the city."

Inside, they used the bathrooms and then grabbed something to eat at the food court. There were a couple of state cops in line at Pizza Hut, so Scott and Cassie veered over to the McDonald's area instead and took the food to go.

Scott knew they would have a lot of explaining to do to the cops and the FBI when they got back to the city. Telling the truth was out of the question, unless he wanted to use this opportunity to reveal to the world that he was Ant-Man, so he needed a version of the events that sounded credible. He was confident that he'd left no evidence of his own presence in the house, but he knew that the crime scene investigators would have a difficult time figuring out how and why a glass of water had exploded in the kitchen.

During the rest of the car ride, Scott and Cassie rehearsed the story they would tell. Scott made her repeat it back to him a few times to make sure they wouldn't contradict each other.

When they got back to the city, it was a little before 9 p.m. For the first part of the plan, they parked the car near an empty, junk-strewn lot in a rough part of Harlem. Scott wiped the car of any prints, though he doubted the police would check it very closely. Scott knew the way Dugan worked: The car was undoubtedly hot, and the plates had been switched. When the car was found—probably not till it got towed on the next street-cleaning day—it would be difficult to connect it to Willie Dugan's crew, much less to Scott.

For the next part of the plan, they walked a few blocks, and then hailed a cab and headed down to the Upper East Side.

In the back of the cab, Cassie leaned with her head against Scott's shoulder and shut her eyes. Was there a better feeling in the world than your daughter falling asleep using your shoulder as a pillow? If there was, Scott hadn't experienced it yet.

As they neared the corner of Seventy-Ninth Street and First Avenue, Scott said to the driver, "Right over here's fine." He nudged Cassie awake and said, "We're here, honey."

They got out of the cab and walked down First.

"I'm so tired, Daddy," Cassie said.

Scott was exhausted, too. He wished it were a normal night—
that he could get into bed and fall asleep reading, knowing that
Cassie was safe in her bedroom. But when they turned onto Seventy-
Eighth Street, and saw the news trucks and police cars and law-
enforcement personnel near his apartment building, he knew the
next round of chaos was about to begin.

FIFTEEN

IN THE living area of Scott's apartment, Agent Warren and Agent James had been questioning Scott and Cassie for at least two hours. Cassie had been examined by EMTs, who determined that she'd suffered no physical injuries during the abduction, although they suggested a psychiatric eval to help her deal with the effects of her experience. Now, as far as Scott was concerned, the questioning by the FBI was causing more trauma for her.

At first Scott had done most of the talking. Then Cassie had given her version of the events, and then Warren and James had gone back and forth asking Scott and Cassie questions—sometimes the *same* questions. It reminded Scott of the times he'd been arrested and interrogated by the police, except this time the questioners weren't trying to catch him in a lie. They had no suspicion at all that Scott and Cassie were lying about anything; they just wanted to make sure they had all the facts straight so they could close their case on Willie Dugan. Cassie had given the agents the address of the house in which she'd been held in Wallkill, and the Feds had already gotten word that local police had discovered the three bodies there.

"Let's run this through one more time," Warren said to Scott, possibly unaware that he'd used the "one more time" line about a half hour earlier. "When did you get the call from Cassie?"

"Is this really necessary?" Scott asked. "My daughter's exhausted, and she's had a difficult day—obviously. And she has to go to school tomorrow."

"Tomorrow's Saturday," James said.

"Oh, that's right." Scott had lost track of the days.

"My poor dad," Cassie said. She smiled; it was good to see her smile again.

"This is the last time," James said. "I promise."

After a deep breath, Scott said, "About four-thirty this afternoon."

"Walk us through what happened after that," Warren said, "and be as detailed as you possibly can."

James, as he'd been throughout the questioning, was taking notes on an iPad.

"There isn't any more detail," Scott said. "I got the call from Cassie that she had escaped from the house. I asked her where she was, and she said Wallkill, New York, and that she'd gone to a coffee bar in town and borrowed a woman's phone to call me. I told her to wait where she was, and then I rented a Zipcar and went to Wallkill. I picked her up, and we drove back to the city. I didn't tell the police about the call because Cassie told me the men had warned her that if the police showed up, she'd be killed. At the time I didn't know the exact situation, so I went up there, picked her up, and drove her back to the city. Oh yeah, and we stopped at a McDonald's, where I called my wife—you can check on that—and I had two Filet-O-Fishes and a vanilla shake, and Cassie had a grilled southwest chicken wrap with a vanilla shake and onion rings. You said you wanted details, right?"

Scott smiled, but the FBI agents didn't seem to enjoy the sarcasm.

"Are you sure you're covering all of the relevant details?" Warren asked.

"Yes, that's all of it," Scott said.

Scott knew there were many details in this story that wouldn't pass a good fact-checking. For example, if Scott had rented a Zipcar, that should show up on a check of his credit-card records. And if Cassie had called him in distress, where was the evidence of the phone call? Scott was hoping that the Feds wouldn't dig into his account too deeply—that they'd be content that Dugan and his crew were dead, off the board, and assume that another associate of Dugan's killed them. As long as the Feds didn't know this had anything to do with Ant-Man, Scott would be happy.

The first time he'd told this story, Agent Warren had lectured him for not reporting the distress call, saying that he could have jeopardized his safety and his daughter's safety—yadda, yadda, yadda. Scott had apologized profusely for his "lapse," claiming that he'd been in shock about the kidnapping and had acted impulsively. He apologized for any trouble he'd caused the police or the FBI.

Yeah, he'd sucked it up big time.

"There's still one thing I don't understand," Warren said.

Uh-oh.

"And what's that?" Scott asked, bracing for another lecture.

"Carlos Torres, the federal marshal, said you went up to your apartment a little before you got the call from Cassie," Warren said. "How did you get out of the apartment building without him seeing you?"

Warren hadn't asked this question yet, and Scott paused, wanting to be careful with his words. "I have no idea. I just walked out the front door."

Scott felt bad for putting Carlos in the awkward position of explaining to his superiors how he'd let Scott slip away.

"The way you and your daughter have been disappearing, you'd think you two were ghosts, or something."

"Ha ha," Scott said nervously. "So are we through with the questioning yet?"

"Don't worry, I won't forget to let you know when we're through," Warren said in the pompous, controlling tone he must have perfected in interrogation training at Quantico. He looked at Cassie and said, "And can you tell me what happened to you one last time?"

Cassie looked exhausted, her eyes bloodshot.

"Come on," Scott said, "is this really necessary?"

"It's okay, Dad," Cassie said.

For the umpteenth time, Cassie explained to Warren and James how she was abducted on First Avenue between Seventy-sixth and Seventy-seventh Street. She described the two kidnappers, as well as she could remember them—the big guy had bushy eyebrows; the short guy was balding.

"Did you see the driver of the car?" Warren asked.

"No, I told you," Cassie said. "It was happening too fast."

"Okay," Warren said. "Continue."

Cassie explained how she was bound and gagged in the car, how they switched cars a few times, and how she'd been taken to the house upstate. She retold an anecdote about a Sherlock Holmes story she'd read in school and said she hadn't known where she was, but thought she was a couple of hours or so from Manhattan. She described being gagged, and the other man who had come to talk to her. This was a part of the story that Scott and Cassie had rehearsed while driving back to the city earlier. Scott had told Cassie it was fine to mention that a third man had come in to speak to her, but that she couldn't say anything about his Ant-Man questions. As in the earlier round of interrogation, Cassie didn't mention anything she wasn't supposed to mention.

Finally, Cassie told the agents about how she'd heard the gunshots in the house, and how terrified she'd been. She was getting visibly upset—shaking, her voice trembling as she spoke.

Angry that Cassie had to be put through retelling this again, for the third or fourth time, Scott cut in with, "There's no reason to make her do this again. Come on."

"He's right," James said.

"Okay, fine," Warren agreed grudgingly. "What about any other people in the house?"

"I told you, I only know about the three men."

"But you said you heard someone leaving? In a car."

"I heard the car, that's it."

"Is there any distinctive smell you remember?"

"The house smelled like Mexican food," Cassie said.

"I mean the odor of a person."

"I told you, I remember how two of the guys smelled. One had strong cologne. The other one smelled like he'd just came back from the gym."

Scott listened, proud of Cassie for answering the questions exactly the way he'd instructed her to answer them, despite her fatigue and how shaken up she was. He'd told her not to mention anything about the fourth guy in the house because he himself didn't understand exactly what had happened to him today—how he had been temporarily paralyzed, and for that purpose. He still didn't believe any of it had been coincidental. Dugan, the two other dead men, and maybe one more person had lured him to the house under the suspicion that Scott was Ant-Man. There might have been some dispute before Scott arrived; in any case, the three men had been killed, perhaps by the same guy who had paralyzed Scott. Or the fourth guy might have arrived later and had nothing to do with the murders.

Scott had no idea what the killer or killers wanted from him, or what the point of paralyzing him was. But if it involved the Ant-Man technology, he had to find out the answer before the Feds did. While Scott knew this could be pure paranoia—that the strange events might have nothing to do with Ant-Man—there was basis for his concern. There had been attempts to steal his technology in the past; in the wrong hands it could be used as a dangerous weapon. What if a drug lord got hold of the tech? Or what if the leader of a rogue country created an army of ant-sized soldiers? The possibilities were practically endless.

There were already reporters camped out in front of the apartment, and the kidnapping and Cassie's dramatic escape was the top news story in New York—maybe all over the country. If the Feds discovered that Ant-Man was involved, and it came out that Scott *was* Ant-Man, there would be an even bigger media circus—and more disruption in Scott and Cassie's lives.

Finally content with the information they'd obtained, Warren and James said goodnight, and left Scott and Cassie alone.

The drama wasn't over. Scott knew that tomorrow there would be more questioning from the Feds, and maybe the NYPD, as additional info about the case came out and the search for Dugan's killer, or killers, progressed. Worse, there would be an onslaught from the media about the case. Those reporters camped out in front of the building hadn't had access to Scott and Cassie yet.

That said, after all of the drama and craziness of the day, it was nice to be alone with Cassie in the apartment.

"So, did I lie well for you?"

Scratch that. Cassie sounded angry, bitter.

Scott listened at the door to make sure the agents were gone, then said, "Come on, don't think of it as lying."

"Oh really? Then what do you call it?"

Scott hesitated, then said, "Being not entirely forthcoming."

"That's your logic," Cassie said. "That's really how you think. When you were stealing, did you say, 'It's not really stealing because I only steal from bad people, or from people who deserve it,' or whatever you could think of to make yourself feel better?"

"Okay, Cassie, you're tired," Scott said. "I get it, but you're going to have to stop all this now and—"

"Your secrets almost got me killed today," Cassie said.

"What?" Scott said. "You're not making any—"

"The whole reason we had to be protected was because that crazy guy, Willie Dugan, was out to get you. And why was he out to get you? Because of the other big secret me and Mom have been keeping for you, and I'm sick of it, totally sick of it. There's always another secret, and another one after that—it's neverending with you. There's always something new I can't do, or can't tell anybody. Why's it always about you and your secrets, anyway? What about me? When do I get to have a life?"

Scott knew this wasn't just teenage melodrama. He'd messed up as a husband and as a father, and she had a right to be upset with him.

"I hear you, Bear," he said, "and I've been trying to settle down, make things more stable for you."

"Don't call me Bear!" She was raising her voice. "You call this stable? I got kidnapped today, I was questioned by the FBI. Everybody in the world, not only in school, knows about me now. You know how embarrassing this is? How *humiliating*?"

Scott was going to remind her that her stealing the Ant-Man suit had caused some of her "instability" lately. But he caught himself, knowing this argument wouldn't hold up since it was *his* suit.

"I'm trying to change things for you," Scott said. "I really am trying."

Cassie glared at him for several seconds, then went into her bedroom and locked the door.

Not surprisingly, the story about the Upper East Side kidnapping and Cassie Lang's dramatic escape from captivity in Wallkill, New York—where the bodies of three men, including one of the country's most wanted fugitives, had been discovered—was the lead story on every major newscast. There was also a report on how the dead man in Louisiana had been identified as Lawrence Mulligan, the retired New York judge who had presided over Dugan's murder trial.

"Great detective work there," Scott said. "Bravo for the FBI."

Lying in bed, in the dark, Scott watched a couple of the network stories. Then he turned to CNN for the more extensive coverage, including repeated footage of the location—and of the law-enforcement personnel, news crews, and curiosity seekers in front of Scott's building. Scott's apartment faced the back, so he couldn't see out to the street at the moment, but he could still hear the commotion.

He fell asleep with the TV on. In the morning, the coverage of the kidnapping was still the big news story. New York 1, the local news station, was showing live footage of the front of Scott's building. It looked to Scott like there were more reporters out there than the night before. This was worse than protective custody—now they were prisoners.

As if on cue, a text arrived from Tony Stark:

Well done my brother

Scott could tell the text was leaking sarcasm. He texted back:

It's not done yet

And he got from Tony:

Seriously, thrilled Cassie is home safe. If you need anything I'm always here for you. You know that.

Scott texted back:

Thanks man! Appreciated!

There was no sarcasm on Scott's part. It gave him a great sense of security to know that as bad as things got in his life, he was never alone; his friends always had his back.

At around eleven a.m., he got a call on his landline from a blocked number.

He picked up and said, "Yeah?"

"Hope you got some rest. It's Agent Warren."

"What's going on?" Scott asked.

"You'll be happy to know the order of protection has been lifted," he said. "You're a free man."

"So you caught the killer from upstate?" Scott asked, wondering why he hadn't heard anything about this on the news yet.

"No, that investigation is ongoing," Warren said. "But the protection order was related to the threat from William Dugan, and that threat has been eliminated."

"Hold up, I'm not following," Scott said. "A killer's out there, somebody who has seen my daughter, may have even been involved in her abduction, and might fear my daughter can ID her. And you say the threat has been *eliminated*?"

Of course, Scott didn't mention that the killer had probably seen him, as well—and, worse, knew he was Ant-Man.

"Yes, that's the situation," Warren said. "But I'm surprised you're upset, given how ambivalent you were initially."

"I'm *not* surprised," Scott said. "This was never about protecting me or my family. This was about you, the FBI."

"Excuse me, but one of our men took a bullet trying to protect your family."

"No, he took a bullet trying to protect your job. You took serious heat when Dugan whacked those guys on your watch, and you didn't want it to happen again."

"So what're you saying?" Warren said. "You *want* protection now?"

Scott wasn't sure what he wanted from the FBI now.

"I just want my daughter to be safe," he said. "How's she supposed to go to school? How she's supposed to go anywhere on her own?"

"As of right now, we don't have any reason to believe you or your family is in danger. If that situation changes, we'll let you know immediately. But for all we know, the murders upstate are an isolated incident that has nothing to do with you or your family. Unfortunately, we can't spend government resources on assumptions. We can only act on facts."

Scott realized that even if the FBI did continue protection of Cassie, that might not help. After all, these people were brazen enough to kidnap Cassie in broad daylight and shoot a federal marshal. If somebody wanted to come after her, putting another marshal on duty wouldn't exactly guarantee her safety.

"I understand the situation. Thanks for everything," Scott said.

He spent the rest of the morning in his tiny apartment, feeling something he hadn't felt in years—like a prisoner at Rykers Island. That had been the darkest time of Scott's life. Being holed up in an apartment on the Upper East Side wasn't exactly like the nightmare of day-to-day life in prison, but he hated the feeling of being trapped, restrained. Since prison, he had often had recurring nightmares of being bound, or confined in small places. One of his favorite things about being Ant-Man was he could never be trapped. It was like his ex-prisoner's fantasy had come to fruition—there was practically no space that could hold him.

But at the moment, Ant-Man wasn't an option. While Scott could easily shrink down and bypass the throngs outside, he couldn't go anywhere without Cassie. He couldn't leave her home alone, unprotected, with a killer possibly after her. And if he left the building with her, they would be swarmed by reporters.

The TV repeated the same news reports about the kidnapping and murders, but there was no mention of any breakthrough in the search for the killer. That didn't mean anything, of course. Even if the cops were closing in on a suspect, the information might not be public yet. Scott was concerned that if the cops captured the killer, the killer would reveal his Ant-Man identity. The bigger issue, though, was what *else* the killer might reveal. What if there had been an ulterior motive for the kidnapping? Scott thought again of the possibility that the killer wanted the Ant-Man tech. Either way, Scott needed to find the murder suspect before the police did.

At noon, Cassie was still sleeping. That was good—Scott was glad she was resting. He decided this would be a good time to suss out the situation with the reporters.

As he approached the vestibule, he was surprised by the sheer volume of people outside. There seemed to be dozens of reporters. When he was spotted, the crowd started calling out his name.

"Hey." George, the super, had approached Scott from behind, startling him. Maybe Scott was suffering post-traumatic stress after being ambushed from behind yesterday.

"This is crazy, huh?" Scott said.

"Maybe you should go away, on vacation," George said. "This is no good for the neighbors."

Sending Cassie away for several days, maybe to Oregon with Peggy, wouldn't have been a bad idea if her safety were guaranteed. But with the protection order ending, Scott couldn't take that risk. And he wasn't going anywhere himself until he found out what exactly had happened to him upstate.

"Sorry for all this," Scott said. "I'm sure it will die down soon."

"It's not dying down, it's getting worse," George said. "This is a violation of your lease. I'm reporting you to the management company. If you don't do something, go away, you're getting evicted."

George's enraged face was bright pink and veins were visible on his forehead. He returned to his apartment and slammed the door.

Scott knew it wouldn't be easy to evict him, but the possibility wasn't so farfetched. Thanks to Willie Dugan, Scott's daughter had been kidnapped, his job was in jeopardy, and he might have to find a new place to live. Scott hadn't exactly done a great job providing stability for Cassie.

Fed up, Scott opened the front door. Reporters rushed forward, holding up microphones and shouting his name and questions. Several TV cameras also were aimed at him.

"Okay, chill," Scott said. "Everybody just chill. I'm going to make one statement and one statement only."

The crowd quieted.

Then Scott said, "I'm thrilled and relieved to have my daughter back home safe. This has been an extremely difficult and taxing time for our family, and I ask that you please respect our privacy. Thank you."

The reporters were shouting questions as Scott went back inside the building. He didn't think that his brief, generic statement would deter the media for very long, but it was worth a shot.

When he arrived back at the apartment, Cassie was awake and at the dining table, having a bowl of cereal and looking at her cell phone. After the hell of yesterday, it was great to see her back to a normal morning routine.

Scott went over to her, kissed her on top of her head the way he'd been doing since she was a baby, and said, "Morning, Sweetie, how did you sleep?"

"Okay," she said, "had a few nightmares."

"You can see that trauma expert they suggested," Scott said. "I'll make an appointment for you."

"Whatever," she said. "I'm sure I'll live."

She took a few last quick bites of cereal, then got up and said, "I gotta get ready."

"Ready?" Scott asked.

"Oh yeah," she said. "I'm gonna go out. You said I could buy a new phone today, right?"

They'd had the conversation about a new phone during the car ride back from upstate.

"I'm afraid going out's impossible right now," Scott said.

"What do you mean?" Cassie asked. "Why?"

He explained the situation with the reporters outside.

"So?" she said. "That doesn't mean I have to stay inside all day."

"It's not a good idea to go out there and deal with all that," Scott said, "especially after what you went through yesterday. We can hang out inside today, and hopefully tonight the crowd will thin out."

"That's crazy," she said. "I'm fine, and I want to see my boyfriend."

"I'm sorry, your *who*?"

"His name's Tucker," she said.

"Oh right, Tucker McKenzie, how could I forget? But since when is he your boyfriend?" Scott wondered, *Did Peggy know about this?* "And I thought kids in school don't have boyfriends and girlfriends."

"What?" She was acting lost. "I don't know what you mean."

"No, that's right—you said nobody *dates* anymore. But I guess that's different from having boyfriends and girlfriends."

"Yeah, it's totally different," she said.

"When did this all happen?" Scott asked. "You've had Roger shadowing you—and trust me, I know what that's like." Now Scott was thinking about his coffee date with Jennifer.

"What difference does it make?" Cassie asked. "It happened, and he wants to meet up with me at Sixteen Handles later." Sixteen Handles was a frozen-yogurt place.

"First of all, I have to meet Tucker McKenzie, or any boy you go out with," Scott said. "Second, I told you, today's a bad day for this. And you probably won't be able to go anywhere alone for a while."

"What do you mean? Why not?"

Scott explained that the protection order had been lifted—but as far as Scott was concerned, it wasn't safe for Cassie to be alone with a killer loose.

"But the FBI thinks it's safe," Cassie said, "or they would still want to keep protecting me, right?"

"Not necessarily," Scott said.

"What do you mean? So now you think you know more than the FBI?"

"Hey, watch it," he said.

"I think it's just because you don't want me to go out with Tucker," she said. "It has nothing to do with wanting me to be safe. If you wanted me to be safe, you would've been protecting me yourself yesterday instead of having the FBI protecting me."

"I saved you," he said.

"Yeah, and I wouldn't've needed to be saved if you weren't Ant-Man, if you were just a normal dad," she said. "It's all your fault, it's *always* your fault, and I'm always getting punished for it."

"Cassie, come on," Scott said, "I know you're upset right now, but—"

"I hate you," she said. "I hate *this*."

She marched into her room and slammed the door. After George, this door-slamming thing seemed to be becoming a trend in Scott's life.

Scott was angry at himself for snapping at Cassie, for losing control. Sometimes he thought he was doomed to make the same mistakes again and again.

The intercom buzzed—someone was in the vestibule. Scott ignored it, figuring it was a reporter trying to get him to come down. More buzzing. After a few minutes of this, Scott's cell rang—a restricted number.

"Yeah?" Scott said into the phone.

"Hey, it's Carlos."

"Hey," Scott said.

"How come you're not answering the buzzer?"

"I thought it was a reporter."

"Lemme up," Carlos said. "It's urgent."

SITTING across from Carlos at the dining table, Scott looked at Carlos's iPad. It showed a picture, extracted from surveillance video, of Scott and the woman with whom he'd had coffee, taken when they were walking together along First Avenue.

"Her name's not Jennifer," Carlos said. "It's Monica. Monica Rappaccini. I checked her out, just on a hunch. Do you know anything about her?"

"Only what she told me at the diner," Scott said. "She moved here from Hoboken, has a daughter."

"All lies," Carlos said. "She has a long rap sheet, and has been associated with several crime organizations, including Hydra and A.I.M."

Scott's first thought: *An ex-con—no wonder I fell for her.* Ex-cons had a way of finding each other, the way alcoholics had a way of finding each other. But he knew this woman's criminal associations had much greater implications.

"I had no idea who she was," Scott said. "What made you look into her?"

"Just seemed suspicious," Carlos said, "her showing up right before your daughter gets kidnapped. Facial recog came up a perfect match." Carlos reached over and thumbed through a few other photos of Scott and Monica, as well as a couple of close-ups of her.

In his head, a montage of the coffee date with Monica un-spooled, including all of the questions about ants. Was this proof that she was working with Dugan and maybe had killed him and the other men?

"Well, that's pretty weird," Scott said. "But what does it have to do with me?"

"You wanna tell me?" Carlos said.

This wasn't "nice Carlos," the federal marshal who'd invited Scott out to the Bronx sometime. This was "hard-ass Carlos" who wanted answers from Scott, not questions.

"Well, it shows that I have really bad judgment in women," Scott said.

Scott smiled, but Carlos wasn't going there.

"Tell me the truth, man," Carlos said. "I'm not playin' right now. I'm already catching heat for letting you out of your apartment building to go upstate. Still don't know how you pulled that off. What are you, some kind of Houdini?"

Scott smirked.

"Seriously," Carlos said. "Did you know about this woman's background?"

"Of course I didn't know that," Scott said. "I thought her name was Jennifer. This is all news to me."

"You don't have any idea why she gave you a fake name?"

"No," Scott said, but he had a hunch. Maybe Jennifer—Mon-ica—had given him a fake name because she'd been trying to figure out whether he was Ant-Man, so she could lure him upstate. Maybe she was the one who'd killed Dugan and zapped him.

But if this were true, what was her motive?

"It's kind of a coincidence," Carlos said, "that she approached you under an alias a couple of days before your daughter was abducted."

"I guess coincidences happen," Scott said.

"Not very often," Carlos said. "Do you think it's possible Monica Rappaccini had anything to do with kidnapping Cassie?"

"I don't know," Scott said.

Carlos was staring at him, as if trying to tell whether he was lying. Scott was trying to keep a straight face, to look innocent—but it didn't help that he *was* lying. Well, partly lying.

"Monica Rappaccini is dangerous," Carlos said. "She's a free agent, has no loyalty, works for whoever's willing to pay her the most. She's a scientist, but we believe she's worked as a thief, smuggler, even an assassin. Basically if anybody's willing to pay her enough for a job, she'll do it."

Scott remembered how he'd been so enthralled with her, even thinking she might be "the one."

"A damn good actor, too," Scott said.

"Did you know about any connection she had to Willie Dugan?" Carlos asked.

"Wait." Scott stared at Carlos, getting upset. "Are you seriously asking me that question?"

Carlos didn't say anything, which meant: yes.

Scott started whispering, so Cassie wouldn't hear in the next room. "My daughter was kidnapped yesterday. If I knew this woman had a connection to Willie Dugan, do you really think I would have had coffee with her and kept it a secret from you?"

"I don't know what you'd do and wouldn't do," Carlos said. "All

I know is you're an ex-con, and you used to be friends with Willie Dugan."

"Not friends," Scott said. "I just worked with the guy. And what's that supposed to mean?"

Scott couldn't believe he'd actually been starting to like this guy.

"Maybe she met with you to send you a message from Dugan, something you didn't want me to know about."

"And I did this knowing I'd put my daughter in danger?"

"Maybe you didn't know about that part," Carlos said. "Maybe they made you some offer, and you turned it down."

"Think about that—just think about that for a second," Scott said. "Why would I do that?"

"So you really didn't know anything about her background?"

"I didn't even know her real name before you came in here and told me."

Carlos shook his head, then got up and started pacing the room.

"I don't know what to believe," he said. His voice sounded weaker, like he was losing conviction, as if he was realizing that his conspiracy theory about Scott didn't make any sense.

Then it hit Scott what was really going on here.

"Wait, I get it now," Scott said. "I get why you're so upset, accusing me of working with Dugan, and why you're coming here on your own. Why wouldn't Warren and James be here if you were supposed to be questioning me? You're here alone because you were already under fire for how I snuck out of the apartment. If your bosses find out you let a known criminal approach me on the street under your watch, it'll cost you your job. So you come in here and throw a Hail Mary, accuse me of working with her, in the hope you can go back to your bosses with a big score and uncover some kind of conspiracy. But it's just a prayer—you don't even believe it yourself."

Carlos stopped pacing and said, "Okay, look—you're right, man, my ass is on the line big time, and you gotta be straight with me now. What did you talk about at that diner?"

Recalling their conversation, mainly about ants, Scott said, "Nothing in particular. Just, uh, small talk."

"Small talk about what?"

"Our work. She told me she's a photographer and lived in Hoboken, but was moving to the Upper East Side."

"What else?"

"We talked about our kids. She said she has a teenage daughter and—wait, she asked me what school Cassie goes to and said her daughter's going to the same school. If she was working with Dugan, maybe that's how she knew where to wait for Cassie after school."

"So you think Monica Rappaccini was in the car with the kidnappers?" Carlos asked.

"No idea," Scott said. "Cassie didn't say she was, but she could've been driving. Cassie couldn't see who was driving the car."

Carlos stared at Scott and said, "Are you hiding something from me, man? You better tell me right now. If these people kidnapped your daughter once, who knows what they'll try next time."

"What're you talking about?" Cassie asked.

She had entered the room without Scott noticing.

"It's nothing, Sweetie," Scott said.

"He said somebody's going to try to kidnap me again," Cassie said.

"That isn't true," Scott said.

"But that's what he said," Cassie said. "I want to know what's going on. I have a right to know what's going on."

Cassie was losing it—shaking, panic in her eyes.

"Okay, just calm down," Scott said.

From there, things went from bad to worse, with Cassie screaming and crying.

At one point, Carlos said, "I'll wait out in the hallway."

Finally, Scott was able to soothe Cassie's fears, convince her that she wasn't in any immediate danger. She went back to her room.

Scott went out to the hallway and stage-whispered to Carlos, "Look, I've answered all your questions. This order of protection is over, so officially you have no reason to be here."

"Sorry your daughter heard that," Carlos said. "I know you had nothing to do with Dugan, and that you didn't know who that woman was. You're a good guy, you love your daughter. But I also know you're not telling me something."

"If I knew something, I'd tell you." Scott hoped he sounded sincere, convincing. He continued, whispering, "Look, maybe it *was* all just a coincidence. Okay, she lied about her name, and it turned out she has a past, but does that mean she has anything to do with Dugan? She could've lied because she was having coffee with me and didn't want to reveal something about herself. It wouldn't be the first time a woman lied to me on a date. One time a woman told me she was single, and I saw her the next day in the park with her husband and kids." Scott knew he was stretching it with this analogy, but he went on, "I'm sure it's just like that. I know you're paranoid about something bigger going on, and it being on you. I'll tell you what—if this Monica gets in touch with me, you'll be the first call I make. I'm not expecting that to happen, though. I think I met a woman, she blew me off, and I'll never hear from her again. Hey, that wouldn't be the first time, either."

Carlos didn't laugh, or even smile, but Scott didn't expect him to. Carlos had to accept the situation—he didn't have any choice.

"Okay," he said. "I appreciate that. Let's stay in touch, man. And don't worry, I won't come over here again uninvited. I promise."

Back in his apartment, Scott felt relieved, but he knew he had to find Monica Rappaccini before Carlos, or anyone at the FBI, did. Otherwise his Ant-Man identity would be revealed, and maybe the technology would be sold to the highest bidder. While Scott wasn't sure whether Monica had been the one who'd zapped him at the house, everything was pointing in her direction.

Just for the hell of it, he went online on his iPad and Googled "Monica Rappaccini" and "criminal." He didn't find anything useful. But when he typed in just "Monica Rappaccini" to Google Images, several photos of her appeared. One was from a high-school reunion in California, taken a few years ago; another was a photo of her and several other women on a beach; the other two seemed to be from a wedding. There was nothing in any of the pictures to indicate that she was living a double life. She seemed so benign in the photos that Scott would have believed Carlos had gotten something wrong, that she wasn't involved with Hydra and A.I.M. at all—if she hadn't told him that photographer-in-Hoboken story the other day. Scott didn't need any proof that Monica Rappaccini was a liar and a scammer—he'd seen the evidence in person.

Scott turned on the TV, then went to check on Cassie, but the door was locked.

"Cassie, open up. I want to talk."

She didn't answer.

He knocked hard a few times and said, "Cassie, come on, are you okay?"

Still no response. He was getting concerned. He didn't think she'd hurt herself, but then again he'd never seen her so distraught and traumatized.

He tried again. Still no response. He was about to shrink to ant size when something on the news caught his attention. It had nothing to do with Willie Dugan. Then again, maybe it did.

Close-up images of bushes with dead ants hanging upside-down from the leaves were shown. The anchorwoman, in a jokey tone, explained that thousands of ants had died in Upstate New York in what appeared to be a mass suicide. There was a closer shot of the dead ants as the anchorwoman said that scientists "don't know what is causing the ant suicides, but think it could be related to the so-called zombie fungus that normally affects ants in South America." She joked to the anchorman next to her that she hoped a "vampire fungus doesn't hit the ants next," and then went on to the next news story.

Scott felt empathy for the ants—all those lives wasted—and anger toward the newscasters for not taking it seriously.

Cassie came out of the bedroom, noticing how upset he was. "Dad, what's wrong? What's going on?"

Scott, distraught, didn't say anything.

SEVENTEEN

SCOTT switched channels frantically, trying to find more information about the zombie ants. But he couldn't find anything.

"What're you looking for?" Cassie asked. "What's wrong? Is it something bad? You're scaring me."

"Yes, it's something bad," Scott said. "Very, very bad."

On the iPad, Scott found a few reports that were pretty much the same as what he'd seen on TV, reporting on the strange ant deaths in "Upstate New York." Then, on another news site, he found what he'd been expecting to find: that the ants were dying mainly in Wallkill, New York.

"I knew it," he said.

"Knew what?" Cassie asked.

Scott scanned the article again as Cassie read it over his shoulder. The stories didn't make any connection between the ant deaths and the murders of Willie Dugan and his crew, but why would they? The only connection—well, the only *obvious* connection—was that both events had taken place in Wallkill.

"Wait, I get it now," Cassie said. "Does this have something to do with all those ants that were near the house when we left?"

Smart kid.

"It might," Scott said.

Scott had summoned all those ants to the house—maybe they'd been affected by something that had happened nearby. Scott flashed back to getting zapped, falling onto his back like a dying bug. Had whatever zapped him also affected the ants?

"But just because ants were there, why are they committing suicide now?" Cassie asked.

"It's not actually suicide," Scott said. "They can't help themselves. I've heard about the zombie ants before. A fungus grows in their brains, and causes them to seek out moist areas and die. This fungus, it's the biggest natural enemy of ants. That's how it got the zombie nickname. It totally sucks the life out of them."

"So a bunch of ants died," Cassie said. "I get you feel bad for the ants, but what's the big deal?"

"Ants are the most important insect in the ecosystem of the entire planet," Scott said. "If all humans were removed from Earth, Earth would be better off. But if all ants were removed, there would be mass extinctions and chaos. You know those dystopian novels you love to read? It would be like that, but worse. Much worse."

"So that's what you think's happening?"

"Honestly, I'm not sure, Cass. All I know is whatever's happening is happening fast. Normally it would take days, even weeks, for the fungus to progress to the point where it would cause mass deaths. So something must've happened, something that accelerated the growth of the fungus or that's causing it to spread."

Scott was talking to Cassie, but he was also talking to himself, thinking out loud.

Then Cassie asked, "But if it's a fungus, where did it come from?"

"It just takes one ant," Scott said. "An ant could've come over in a crate of fruit from South America and wound up in Wallkill. When I called to the ants for help, the infected ant could have been one of them, one of thousands. Normally, ants have defenses, so whatever happened must've messed with the immunity of the ants. But why would they want do that? What do they get out of it?"

"Who's they?" Cassie asked.

"I don't know," Scott said. "That's the problem." He realized he'd said too much. He didn't want to frighten her again.

"Never mind," Scott said. "Can you get dressed to go out?"

"I thought you said we can't go out today."

"We have no choice now. Come on, get ready, let's go."

As Cassie was getting dressed in her room, Scott's mind was churning, trying to figure out what Dugan's and maybe Monica Rappaccini's motive was in all this. It was like trying to solve a complicated riddle. He knew the answer was there, that it existed, but that made it even more frustrating that he couldn't come up with it. Why did they want to destroy the ant population in the area? Was it some sort of sadistic, nihilistic payback plan by Dugan? The world had screwed him over, so he was going to screw the world?

No, that didn't make sense. Dugan had wanted revenge, yes, but for him revenge was always personal. Was it about money? That didn't make sense, either. Where was the money in a potential ant holocaust?

On the NY1, the anchorman said, "The unexplained suicide-like deaths of ants in Upstate New York appears to be expanding. There are a reports of the mass deaths of ants throughout the Catskills and Adirondacks, into parts of Pennsylvania and Connecticut."

Scott had heard enough. He shouted, "Come on, right now!" He practically grabbed Cassie and pulled her out of the apartment.

Cassie was holding her jacket as Scott raced down the stairs. There weren't as many reporters and onlookers in front of the building as there had been earlier, but there were enough people to cause a tumult when Scott and Cassie exited.

"Keep walking—don't say anything to anybody," Scott instructed Cassie as they made their way along the sidewalk, heading toward York Avenue. A couple of cops helped clear a path for them; when they got to the corner, only a few reporters were still trailing them, shouting questions.

Scott hailed a cab heading downtown and got in with Cassie.

"Fifty-seventh and Sixth," Scott said to the driver. "As fast as you can."

"There's gonna be bridge traffic," the driver said. "I can't fly, buddy."

"Are you gonna tell me where we're going?" Cassie asked Scott.

"*We're* not going anywhere," Scott said. "I'm taking you someplace you'll be safe."

"No, let me out!" Cassie screamed.

She reached for the door as the cab started moving, and Scott had to grab her hand to prevent her from opening it.

The driver stopped short, wide dark eyes glaring in the rearview, and said, "Hey, you crazy back there? Want to get killed?"

"It's okay," Scott said. "Drive, just drive." Then he said to Cassie, "Look, I swear you won't be in any danger."

"Yeah," Cassie said, "that's what you said last time."

"No, that's what the FBI said the last time."

"I want to come with you, Dad. Please."

"No, Cassie."

"But I can help you. If you think what's happening with the ants has to do with what happened in the house, you need me with you, because I was there!"

"No, absolutely not, it's going to be way too dangerous."

"Oh, really?" Cassie sassed. "And where's it going to be *less* dangerous?"

Scott didn't answer. But about five minutes later, the cab pulled up in front of Stark Tower, Tony's new, obnoxiously large multi-story residence.

"Seriously?" Cassie said. "You want to leave me with Iron Man?"

As they rode the elevator up, Cassie continued to complain. "I don't want to stay here," she said repeatedly. "Why do I have to?" Scott could hardly believe it. Cassie had grown up as a super hero's daughter, which hadn't always been easy for her, but was she so jaded that she was seriously complaining about having hang time with Tony Stark? What if Spider-Man wanted to spend a day with her? Would her attitude be, *Sorry, Spidey, but I'm way too busy for you?*

"You know, in another context, I'd say you're acting spoiled," Scott said.

Scott and Cassie had been announced by the doorman. When they rang the apartment door, which was practically as big as the one in Emerald City, Pepper Potts answered.

Scott hadn't seen her in a while, maybe a few months, and she looked great with her straight red hair and bright green eyes. Had she gotten into Pilates or yoga? He'd had a crush on her when she first started working for Tony, but he backed off when he picked up that she and Tony had something going on between them—he didn't want to get into an awkward love triangle. For a long time,

Tony's relationship with Pepper had been ambiguous. Were they coworkers? Friends? Lovers? Given that she was at Tony's place on a Saturday afternoon, barefoot, in jeans and a T-shirt—it seemed as if she and Tony were officially a couple.

"Wow, it's great to see you guys," Pepper said. She kissed Scott on the cheek, then said to Cassie, "Look at you, you get bigger every time I see you." Then to Scott, she deadpanned, "Wish I could say the same for you."

Little good-natured ant humor there. Scott was used to it.

Then Tony entered in faded jeans, a tight black T-shirt, and five -hundred-dollar designer sneakers—the rich-guy casual look. The outfit said, *I have so much money, I don't have to dress up.*

"Scott, the man," Tony said.

He came over and gave Scott a big hug.

Then Tony said to Cassie, "And look at you, all grown up and pretty. You sure this guy's your dad?"

Nobody was smiling except Tony.

"We need to talk," Scott said.

Picking up on the urgency, Tony said to Pepper, "Hey, Pep, can you take Cassie upstairs, maybe play some dress-up with her?"

"Certainly," Pepper said.

"Dress-up?" Cassie asked, as she reluctantly followed Pepper up the winding staircase.

"We don't want to define anything yet," Tony said to Scott, responding to the unasked question about his relationship with Pepper.

"We, or you?" Scott asked with a slight smirk.

Tony hit back with, "Maybe we can go for a double date sometime. I mean, if you ever have a date again."

"Do you know anything about a woman named Monica Rappaccini?"

Tony paused, processing the question. Then he said, "I know you're not dating her. I mean, even you aren't desperate enough to go out with a nutjob like her." Tony saw Scott's guilty expression. "Or are you?"

"It was just one date," Scott said, "and—"

"Come on, buddy," Tony said, "there have to be better options for you out there. I know you're divorced, and it hurts, but you should be more like me."

"Cold?" Scott asked.

"Practical," Tony said. "When your heart's already broken, you can't get it broken again."

"So what do you know about her?" Scott asked.

"Actually, she's been out of the game for years," Tony said. "Lying low, I guess. She used to work with A.I.M., though, had a scientific background. She knows how to fight, too. Ex-Marine. Changed teams after the war—delusional, felt her country had let her down. Talk about abandonment issues."

Scott explained about getting zapped at the house upstate, and that he suspected Monica had been involved.

When Scott was through talking, Tony, who had remained expressionless throughout, said, "Wow, your life is freaky. I mean, I'm glad I just have shrapnel in my heart and fly around in an electrically powered suit of armor—I feel normal in comparison."

Scott said, "Ants are dying at an incredible rate, committing virtual suicide."

"I heard about that on the news," Tony said. "They're calling it 'Antpocalypse.'"

"I don't think you get the implications of all this," Scott said.

"I get that a bunch of your ant friends are kicking the bucket, and you feel bad about it."

"It's bigger than that," Scott said. "Much bigger. This isn't the beginning of a world war, or an attack from outer space, but it's potentially just as dangerous—if not more so."

Tony was catching on that Scott was serious about all this.

"Continue," Tony said.

"If the ant deaths reach a tipping point," Scott explained, "it'll lead to chaos—we're talking food shortages and mass extinctions."

Now Tony seemed to be getting the direness of the situation.

"Ants are your department, so I defer to you, my friend," Tony said. "What type of time frame are we looking at?"

"Ants are already dying in three states," Scott said. "By the end of the weekend, it could be the entire East Coast."

"And how is this happening so quickly?"

"I'm not sure," Scott said. "I know the ants' immunity has been affected. And I'm almost certain it's related to what happened to me yesterday."

"Obvious question," Tony said. "Why would someone want to kill off the world's ants?"

"I think it was an accident," Scott said. "What's happening to the ants is collateral damage. They wanted something from me, from my Ant-Man tech, and the ants were there. Then somebody double-crossed Dugan, and killed him and the rest of his crew before I got there."

"That sounds like Monica Rappaccini," Tony said. "If she wants something bad enough, she'll do anything to get it. Was that on her dating profile?"

Scott ignored the dig. He said, "And whatever she wants has to be worth a lot of money, or they wouldn't have shot a federal marshal and pulled off a risky kidnapping to get it—and she wouldn't have killed three men and left the evidence."

"So what do you want from me?" Tony asked. "You want me to help you find Rappaccini to figure out what's going on?"

"No, I want something much more important than that," Scott said. "I want you to watch my daughter."

"Sorry?" Tony asked.

"You said you'd help me any time I asked for it," Scott said. "Well, this is the help I need. I can handle Rappaccini, but Cassie's the most important thing in my life, and I can't risk anything happening to her again. Protective custody is over, and I need her to be in the safest possible place. If you can't protect her, who can?"

"You got yourself a deal," Tony said, smiling. "And if you want to find Monica, you also probably want to talk to Peter Lawson. I can give you his address in Brooklyn."

"Who's Peter Lawson?" Scott asked.

"Monica's ex," Tony said. Then, putting on some street affect, he added, "Face it, my man. You got played."

LEAVING Tony Stark's building, Scott reflected that he had to get better at this whole post-divorce-dating thing.

Scott's phone chimed—a restricted number, which he assumed was the FBI.

"Scott, where are you?" Carlos asked.

Walking fast along 57th street, weaving between the horde of tourists, Scott asked, "What's going on?"

"They know you didn't rent a Zipcar to go upstate," Carlos said. "They want to talk to you again."

Scott knew "they" meant agents Warren and James.

"Tell them I can't right now."

"You don't get it. They think you're a suspect now in the murders upstate."

Scott saw a couple of cops up the block. They hadn't seen him, but he did a one-eighty just in case and headed toward Sixth Avenue.

"Tell them to back off," Scott said.

"I can't do that," Carlos said.

"If you want me to find Monica Rappaccini and keep your job, you will," Scott said.

"Did you talk to her yet?" Carlos asked.

Scott ended the call.

He rushed over a few blocks to a diner and went into the bathroom. He took off his street clothes, put them into the pouch attached to his uniform, then activated the Pym gas and was suddenly ant-sized.

He noticed a few ants in the bathroom: two babies and one adult female. They weren't here because they were attracted to Scott—they were obviously sick. They were walking unsteadily and had gross deformities on their heads, as if they'd contracted the ant version of the Elephant Man's disease. They seemed unaware of Scott's presence as they wandered toward the puddle of water under the sink, attracted to the moisture.

Then Scott noticed a few other ants, already dead, next to the pipe. The fungus was spreading even faster than he'd feared.

Scott slipped under the bathroom door and went back out to the busy sidewalk, slaloming between all of the gigantic shoes. Then he hopped on the back of a cab, heading toward Brooklyn. He had to find Monica Rappaccini as soon as possible and hope his hunch was right—that she had caused the zombie fungus epidemic, and that it could be reversed. But with ants now dying in Manhattan, one thing was certain: Time wasn't on anyone's side.

EIGHTEEN

CASSIE had never been impressed with celebrities, maybe because she'd grown up around so many famous super heroes. When she was ten years old, her father had Spider-Man make a surprise visit to her birthday party at a Pizzeria Uno. The other kids thought it was the coolest thing in the world, but to her it was just like, whatever.

Take Tony Stark, for example. Cassie had known him for so long that she didn't even think of him as Iron Man—he just seemed like her crazy uncle. Okay, maybe crazy was a strong word—eccentric. Yeah, he was like her eccentric uncle. Actually, she thought he was kind of annoying. Yeah, his armored suit was cool, and he could do cool things like fly, but she didn't get what was so awesome about him as a person. He was funny, sort of, but he was *so* into himself. Seriously, if he wasn't an egomaniac, why did he have his name on everything in the city? Stark Industries, Stark Tower, Stark Hotel, Stark Ice Skating Rink. If he gave the city enough money, they'd probably rename the Brooklyn Bridge, call it The Stark Bridge. And instead of the Statue of Liberty, it would be the Starktue of Liberty.

Cassie had always liked Pepper, though. She was super-cool and pretty, and Cassie didn't know why she was wasting her time with Tony. Well, Tony was one of the wealthiest men in the world, so

Cassie understood that part, but Pepper didn't seem like the type who would be into a man just because of his money. That was one of the things that Cassie liked best about her. There were rich boys in Cassie's school, boys who lived on Park Avenue and all that, and they always talked about their fancy trips—except they didn't say "trips," they said "vacationing." When Christmas break had come up last year, Cassie heard one Park Avenue boy ask somebody, "Where are you vacationing this year?" It was so annoying. If Pepper were Cassie's age, and they went to school together, Cassie bet they would've hung out and been friends. Maybe not best friends, but friends.

While Cassie's dad and Tony were talking about their super-private saving-the-world stuff that was way too important for her to hear about—eyes rolling—Pepper hung out with Cassie. First Pepper showed Cassie a bunch of dresses that she didn't wear anymore and said that Cassie could have them if she wanted. She tried them on, but Pepper was a few inches taller than her so they didn't fit, which sucked because a few of them were really cute and Cassie had already been imagining wearing one of them on her first real date with Tucker McKenzie. Cassie told Pepper all about Tucker. It was nice to have somebody to talk to, like a woman, with her mother so far away. She obviously couldn't talk to her dad about boys. He was always prying into her life, reading her private texts out loud, trying to embarrass her. Maybe he was only being overprotective like a lot of dads, and she knew that he loved her, but she just wanted to keep everything to herself even more whenever he acted like that.

After they were done trying on clothes, Pepper said she had to go to a hairdressing appointment, so she parked Cassie in front of the TV in the "theater room" of the apartment. The screen was as big as the ones in small theaters, and there were reclining movie-theater-style seats. It was really cool, but Cassie felt like a total baby. She didn't feel like watching a movie, so she flipped channels, stopping at some news story about the Antpocalypse. Wow, it was just like her dad had said—or worse. Ants were dying all over the Northeast. The images of ants, hanging dead from leaves and wherever, were so sad. Cassie remembered how cool it had been to wear the Ant-Man suit the other day, and to see ants from so close up. She hoped her dad figured out what was happening soon, but he'd seemed confused about the whole thing himself, so she wasn't confident.

While she was watching TV, Tucker texted her:

can we hang out later?

She could have been on a date with the cutest boy in school, the love of her life, and instead she was being held prisoner in Tony Stark's home theater. It so wasn't fair.

After about twenty more minutes of boredom and frustration, Tony entered and said, "How's everything going?"

"Terrible," Cassie said.

"At least it's not disastrous or unbearable," Tony said. "I always like to look at the bright side."

"Can I go out for just an hour?" Cassie asked.

"First of all, I promised your dad you wouldn't go anywhere," Tony said. "Second, no."

Tony had his usual arrogant smirk.

"Please," Cassie said. "We won't leave the block, I promise."

"Ah, let me guess," Tony said. "First boyfriend."

"Did Pepper or my dad tell you something?"

Cassie didn't think Pepper had said anything, but she could totally see her dad blabbing about it.

"Nope, just my brilliant intuition," Tony said.

"You can't make me stay here," Cassie said.

"As your very overqualified babysitter, I think I can. And while I know nothing about this charming suitor of yours, if he's anything like the average fourteen-year-old boy—or, god forbid, like I was when *I* was fourteen—he isn't worth it."

"He's fifteen," Cassie said, "and why would I take relationship advice from you? Mr. Never Been Married, Mr. Never Been Serious. And don't tell me it's because you're too busy for a relationship, because that's just a lame excuse."

"Saving the world does tend to take up a lot of a guy's time," Tony said.

"Seriously," Cassie said, "how come you and Pepper won't get married, already? She's so awesome."

"Finally we agree on something," Tony said.

"And you're old—"

"Hey, easy now."

"Older than my dad, anyway," Cassie finished. "I think I know what the problem is."

"Pray tell," Tony said.

"Commitment phobia," Cassie said. "A lot men have it, especially men your age who've never been married."

Tony smiled, said, "Wait, so now *you're* giving *me* relationship advice?"

"Somebody's gotta give it to you," Cassie said, "before you totally blow what you have going on with Pepper. If you wanted to get married, you would've done it by now. It's so obvious she's totally into you. You're just leading her on, making empty promises, and it's not right. If you weren't so into your image and naming buildings after yourself, maybe you'd realize it."

There was a long pause as Cassie and Tony had a staring contest.

Then Tony said, "Well, this has been a blast so far. I wish your dad would leave you here more often. I'd be so psychologically well-adjusted if I just had your guidance."

"Also, your sarcasm," Cassie said. "Obvious defense mechanism probably related to deep-seated insecurity. I'd suggest losing it. Trust me, no woman's going to stick around for that cocky crap especially not one as cool as Pepper."

Tony was impressed with her comebacks. "You're a good kid, Cassie Lang. I won't hold your opinions against you. Want to come upstairs and see something cool?"

Cassie was glad just to get out of this home theater—it was making her claustrophobic—so she followed Tony up to the top floor of the gigantic penthouse.

This was Tony's workspace, where all of the Iron Man magic happened. In the center of the room was one of his gold-and-red Iron Man suits.

"Say hello to my latest toy," Tony said.

Celebrities didn't impress Cassie, but technology blew her away.

"So cool!" She went closer to it and peered inside at the control panel. "Can I go for a ride in it?"

"And you think *I'm* cocky?" Tony said, smiling.

"There's a difference between confidence and cockiness," Cassie said. "Come on, my dad lets me use his suit."

"He does?"

"Well, once, the other day. And he didn't exactly let me, but nothing bad happened."

"That's nice you're so, well, close with your dad," Tony said. "But at Tony Stark's house, only Tony Stark gets to play with the toys."

Cassie, looking at the back of the suit now, said, "Repulsors—nice."

"Yep," Tony said, "they aid in horizontal—"

"—and vertical thrust," Cassie said. "But it's the gyro-stabilized repulsion that makes you fly." She squatted to look at the boots. "Micro-turbines for air liquification, running on rings of liquid nitrogen."

Tony, impressed, asked, "You're into theoretical mechanics, huh?"

"I guess it's just a hobby," Cassie said. "My dad never told me how the Ant-Man technology works, though. I guess he's paranoid about it or something. I had to figure a lot of it out on my own."

"All kidding aside," Tony said, "you have a great dad. You know that, right?"

"Yeah, I know," Cassie said. "One thing I couldn't figure out while I was in the suit is how he can communicate with ants. When I was wearing the suit, it was, like, weird. I felt like I was talking to the ants, but I wasn't talking. It's hard to explain, but it felt like, I don't know, telepathy."

"That's because it probably *is* telepathy," Tony said. "Your dad hasn't shared everything with me, either, and vice versa. Call it super-hero trade secrets, if you will. But if I were guessing, I'd say Hank Pym used a type of synthetic telepathy in the suit. It's how brains can communicate with machines via direct neural interface, except he figured out a way to go from brain to ant."

"But how is that possible?" Cassie asked. "I mean, ants don't think the way people do."

"Exactly," Tony said. "This telepathy is driven by thoughts, not language. Think of a dog whistle, or the way birds communicate. Do they need words or thoughts, or is it really just instinct? I'm guessing your dad can communicate with ants via a similar mechanism, except it's silent—at least to human ears."

"Wait." An idea was coming to Cassie; she was getting excited. "My dad was concerned about me being in the suit because he thought I wasn't old enough, my brain wasn't fully developed. He was worried about me shrinking, what effect it would have on me."

"Call me crazy, but that sounds like a reasonable concern," Tony said.

"But what if it actually worked the *other* way?" Cassie said. "What if my brain did something to the suit? I'm not an adult yet, and the suit has never had a teenage brain in it. When I was communicating with the ants through the direct neural interface, maybe I changed something in the suit, and it, like, opened a portal."

"I'm not following you," Tony said.

"My dad thinks something happened to the ants, something that affected their immunity and let this fungus spread. But maybe it's because the Ant-Man suit sent some kind of signal to the ants. Not on purpose, but because something in the helmet changed to work with my brain."

"He said he thinks their immunity was compromised," Tony said. "If his suit can communicate with the brains of ants, why not with their immune systems?"

"Right," Cassie said, "but if the suit sent a message that altered the immunity of ants, why can't it send one to fix it? We have to tell my dad about this. Where is he now?"

"He'll be back soon."

"We should tell him now, Tony, before the Antpocalypse gets any worse."

"And how are we supposed to do that?" Tony asked. "He's not an easy man to track down. I mean, the guy's the size of an ant."

Actually, Cassie knew exactly how to track down her dad, but she was afraid Tony wouldn't let her leave to go find him. It had been a mistake to even suggest the idea.

"Yeah, you're probably right," she said. "Never mind."

"He'll contact us soon, I'm sure," Tony said.

To change the subject, Cassie asked Tony questions about the Iron Man suit. It totally worked—he loved showing her all of the latest gadgetry. She'd thought her dad was the biggest technology geek in the world, but Tony was just as absorbed.

Later, after Tony had turned on some awful, old heavy-metal music and was busy adjusting something in the turbines, Cassie slipped away to go to the bathroom. Then she realized: She could just leave the apartment. First, she grabbed an iPad, then she took the elevator down to the lobby and strolled past the doorman, and she was free. Tony might have been one of the most powerful super heroes on the planet, but he was the world's worst babysitter.

A few months ago, Cassie had downloaded a GPS tracking app onto Scott's phone. Kids needed to keep tabs on their parents these days, or there was no chance of having any fun. She found a Starbucks with Wi-Fi and connected to Scott's phone via an app she downloaded to the iPad. A map of New York appeared; she zoomed in on Brooklyn and the blue dot near downtown where Scott currently was.

Cassie had five dollars on her—more than enough to buy a single-fare MetroCard at the 57th Street Station at Sixth Avenue. She compared the map on her phone to the subway map and figured that Scott was near the Lafayette Avenue stop on the C train. She took the F downtown to West Fourth and switched for the C. When she arrived at Lafayette, she went up to the street and saw she'd been off, but only by a few blocks. She walked up the avenue to the street and headed toward her dad's location.

It was a normal-looking old house, wedged between two other old houses. There was a short gate in front of it and a bunch of garbage cans. Near an entrance to the basement, lower down, there was a big puddle; it looked like there had been a flood or something in the basement. There were also footprints of water leading up to the house, so someone was probably inside. She had no idea why her dad had gone to this house, or what this had to do with zombie ants, but whatever.

Cassie rang the bell, but no one answered. She tried a few more times; still no answer. She checked the app—her dot was practically on top of her dad's. She tried the handle, and the door was open, so she went inside into the long vestibule near the kitchen. There was a weird, loud buzzing sound in the house—but was it one sound or a bunch of sounds?

"Hello," she called. "Anybody home?"

As she went farther into the house, the buzzing got louder.

NINETEEN

SCOTT, ant-sized, jumped off a van at the intersection of Washington and Fulton, and then darted along the sidewalk. When he got to the house around the corner, he slipped under the door. There were shoes near the door and a pair of boots, all men's. He paused near the staircase, but he didn't hear anything. He went into the kitchen. There was no one in there—well, no one except a mouse puttering near the baseboard of the sink. Although Scott had been Ant-Man for a long time now, and felt as comfortable in miniature as he did when he was normal size, it still always gave him a little jolt when he saw an animal or a bug from his tiny perspective. The mouse didn't notice him at all, though, as he went through the kitchen into the dining room.

Nothing looked out of the ordinary—a table, chairs. He leapt onto the table and saw a mug with steaming coffee inside, indicating that someone was home—or had been recently.

Back on the floor, he crossed into the living room, traversing an Afghan rug that had lots of hairs in it—some of which looked similar to Monica Rappaccini's hair. A door led to the backyard patio. He went outside and saw several ants walking unsteadily, seeming dazed. One of the ants had grotesque growths on its head.

He went back into the house and saw a stack of magazines on the end table near the couch. He climbed up to the top one, a *National Geographic* with a cover story titled—would you believe it?—"Ants of the Amazon." The mailing address that appeared on the label was for Peter Lawson, confirming that Scott had the right address. He was about to go check out the upstairs when he heard footsteps above him, creaking on the wooden floor. Then he heard a woman talking—it sounded like she was on the phone, finishing up a conversation:

"Yeah…okay, I will…thank you…okay…bye."

It sounded like Monica.

Scott moved over near the stairwell as the woman came down-stairs. From his vantage point, he could only see her legs as she arrived at the bottom and walked straight toward him. He moved very close to the wall so she wouldn't notice him. She passed by and went into the living room.

Humming some song Scott didn't recognize, she dropped her cell phone on the coffee table. Then she went into the kitchen and screamed.

The mouse, Scott realized.

"Disgusting," Monica said. "My god!"

Scott came around so he could see Monica, who had backed away from the sink in fear. It was hard to believe that this innocent-looking, mouse-fearing woman was a dangerous criminal who'd hooked up with Willie Dugan's crew—that she'd committed the murders in Wallkill.

"Hey, Monica," Scott said.

Already jittery about the mouse, Monica glared toward the dining room and said, "Who's there?"

Scott stood off to the side of the entrance where he couldn't be seen. He said, "I'm surprised you forgot me so quickly."

Peering around the kitchen, he saw that Monica was holding a large knife.

"Whoever you are, get out now," she said.

Scott dashed into the room, leaped up, and knocked the knife out of Monica's hand.

She was stunned.

Scott landed on the countertop. "I think you're starting to catch on."

She turned and ran out of kitchen. Scott jumped after her, grabbed part of her shirt, and spun her around, pressing her up against the wall.

"It's over now," Scott said. "You're going to be arrested."

He let go of her, dropping to the floor so she couldn't see him.

"I-I have no idea what you're talking about," she said, her eyes shifting back and forth.

"But you know who I am," Scott said. "You know I'm Ant-Man."

"I don't know anything."

Had Scott gotten it all wrong?

He kept going with it. "You killed three men," he said. "They were wanted killers themselves, but you still killed them—and you also did something to the ants."

"You...you're crazy," she said, backing away.

She was looking around frantically, trying to figure out where he was. "You're making a big mistake. I-I have no idea who you are, or what you want from me."

"You wanted my tech," Scott said. "But what for? What do you want to do with it?"

She said, "I have no idea why—" Then she turned, suddenly

making a dash for the living room. Scott was on her right away; he grabbed her from behind. But she held up a tiny device, like something a speaker might use to flip through slides during a video presentation. Scott lost his grip on her back, and he fell straight down to the floor, bouncing, then spinning, with no control of his movements. He lay on his side, unable to move, like at the house in Wallkill.

"Ah, there you are," she said.

Dazed, but uninjured from the fall, Scott saw the gigantic Monica crouching in front of him.

"Silly, Scott," she said. "You really thought you could come in here and stop me all by your little ant-self, with no help from your super-hero friends? Do you have any idea who you're dealing with?"

She picked him up and squeezed him between her thumb and forefinger.

"Wow, Dr. Pym certainly knows what he's doing." She moved in closer. "Look how tiny your head is. And your eyes! I wish I could keep you as my pet. Just walk around with you in my pocket."

Scott had always been cool in a crisis, even during his time as a criminal. He needed to buy time to figure out his next move—if he had a next move. He said, "How do you know Dr. Pym?"

"I don't know him personally," Monica said. "I was a tech geek growing up. I was a fan of his work, but my hero was Einstein. I wanted to create the next super-weapon. But I knew about the so-called Ant-Man, and that he chose someone to follow in his legacy. So it *has* been you all along. I can't believe it—I'm holding Ant-Man right in my hand. How powerful do you feel now, Scott? I'm guessing not so much."

Scott figured it would be a good idea to placate her, seeing as he couldn't move and he was one-thousandth her size. "Yep, at the moment I feel pretty...um...small."

"Small?" She laughed. "Yes, you *are* small. You're also weak, and powerless. And you're about to be dead."

Scott remembered how much he'd liked Monica—Jennifer, then—when he'd first met her. He really knew how to pick 'em.

"So you *were* at the house upstate?" Scott asked, trying to buy time.

"Yes, it was *moi*," she said. "And yes, I killed those three imbeciles."

"How did you hook up with Willie Dugan?" Scott asked.

"Please," she said. "Don't use the term 'hook up.' I met Willie—or Will, as I called him—years ago. We stayed in touch over the years, and he contacted me last week. He was planning to kill you and wanted my help getting out of the country afterwards. I have a lot of connections." She laughed. "It's kind of funny: If I hadn't agreed to help him, you'd already be dead. I guess I bought you another week of life."

"How did he think he'd kill me when I was under protection?"

"He killed those other guys, including that judge," she said. "Trust me, you were next on his list—and he was planning to kill your ex and your daughter, too. He had a big plan in the works, and he would've figured out how to pull it off. But then he told me a story about how you'd once saved his life in a fire. He thought you might be Ant-Man. That's when I made a new deal with him, a deal to get us a ton of money. All I had to do was confirm that you were Ant-Man—and you made that so easy for me at the diner with all that ant talk."

"Okay, so what's your big plan?" Scott said. "Might as well tell me."

Monica was walking around the room now, getting off on the power of holding the tiny, immobilized Scott in the palm of her hand.

"This is nice," she said. "I like this. Much more intimate than our first date at the diner. But it was cute how obviously infatuated you were with me. In another lifetime, we could have been so happy."

"Nah, I don't think so," Scott said. "In a lifetime I would've caught on that you were a worthless psycho and brought you to justice."

She smiled. "Maybe I am worthless. But trust me—you're worth a lot. You would die before I had a chance to kill you, if you heard how much A.I.M. offered to pay me for your ant-communication technology."

"What do they want the technology for?"

"You would have to see it to believe it. It was a brilliant plan, but we had to figure out how to get you to show up somewhere as Ant-Man. Part one was using your smart-ass daughter as bait to lure you upstate as Ant-Man. After I got rid of the dead weight, all I had to do was wait for you to show up. That turned out to be super-easy. First I paralyzed you—then I replicated you."

"Replicated? What do you mean, replicated?"

"I invented a device that can duplicate certain types of technology. Dr. Pym would be proud."

"You replicated my whole suit?"

"No, only what was most valuable," she said. "The ability to communicate with ants. To me, that was Dr. Pym's most impressive invention—only I don't think he took it far enough. If you can control ants, why not other insects? And if you can control other insects, why not animals? And if animals, why not humans?" She was pacing faster, becoming more maniacal. "Think about it. A single person could control an entire army, or force a country to submit without firing a single shot."

"That sounds like a great goal," Scott said sarcastically.

"It *is* a great goal," she said, missing—or ignoring—the sarcasm.

"And you say you were a fan of Dr. Pym's?" Scott said. "Well, I know Pym personally, and he absolutely wanted the technology to be used for good, not evil."

"Who cares about good and evil?" Monica said. "I'm not using the tech, I'm selling it to A.I.M. for...wait for it...twenty million dollars. Whoops, did I let that slip?"

"That's nice," Scott said. "Well, in case you've been living under a rock for the past twenty-four hours, your grand plan has had a grand side effect. Your replicator seems to have caused a fungus mutation that's killing off ants all over the Northeast, maybe beyond."

She stopped pacing, moved her face close to Scott—she was only about an inch away—and said, "Oh, Scott, don't you get it? I don't care about ants. I care about money."

"I don't think *you* get it," Scott said. "If the ants die, everything dies. Well, most things. It won't be a world you'll want to live in."

"I'll have my own island by then," she said.

"Yeah," Scott said, "and you'll be starving to death on it."

"If anybody will be able to afford food, it'll be me."

There was no reasoning with her.

"Is Lawson here?" Scott asked. "Is he in on this, too?"

"Oh, he had an unfortunate accident last week: body hasn't been discovered yet. I'm coming into a lot of money soon, and—if you haven't figured it out yet—I don't play well with others. It's been that way for a long time, since I was a kid. I was the loner type—and, yes, I killed animals. So cliché, I know. But if I could kill all the cats in my neighborhood, you think I care about what's going on with some stupid little ants?"

The ants insult, in particular, made Scott seethe. But he reined it in.

"Well, I have things to do," she said. "It's been nice chatting with you."

She carried him into a small bathroom. Monica lifted the lid to the toilet and, between her thumb and forefinger, held him over the bowl. It looked like he was about to be dropped into a very large, ovular swimming pool.

"Wait—before you kill me," Scott said, "promise me you'll try to reverse what you did. You don't want this ant fungus to spread. It doesn't get you anything."

"It gives me leverage," she said. "Power."

"It's senseless," Scott said, but she wasn't listening.

"Sayonara, Ant-Man."

She dropped him into the bowl.

He landed with what seemed like a big splash and sunk partway into the water. Then there was a tremendous roar, and the water began to swirl. Being flushed down a toilet alive was not an experience Scott had ever expected to have, and it wasn't exactly pleasant. The water churned around, faster and faster. With seemingly incredible force, like the water from a tsunami getting sucked out to sea before the big wave strikes, Scott was sucked down the drain into total darkness.

It felt like being on a roller coaster—a water-ride version of Space Mountain—minus all the fun. The positive was that the water would temporarily disable the suit, reverting him back to his normal size; he just hoped that happened after he reached the sewer, because he wasn't sure what would happen if he suddenly got hundreds of times bigger while he was inside a narrow pipe.

In an ultimate example of *careful what you wish for*, Scott landed with a splash, or a thump, in the city sewer—in an experience he intended to block out from his memory for the rest of his life.

One piece of good news—the paralysis was gone. The Pym gas activated, returning him to human size. Still, he was trapped in a sewer, in total darkness. He felt around, trying to find some way out. Finally, he was able to grab onto something slimy and climb up the concrete ledges along the sewer wall, heading toward faint light. It turned out to be a manhole cover. He managed to unlock it and climbed out of the sewer, up to the middle of the street in front of Monica's house.

Then he realized that a couple of kids on their bikes were watching him in awe. Or maybe shock. It wasn't every day that you saw a super hero emerge from a city sewer.

"Go home," Scott said. "Pretend you never saw this."

Yeah, right, like there was a chance of that. One kid took out his phone and aimed it at Scott for several seconds. Then the kids took off in unison, speeding away up the block. Scott knew it wouldn't be long until that shot was online, if it wasn't already.

Scott approached Monica's house, still drenched and smelling awful. The Ant-Man suit was functioning again, though. He activated the Pym gas, shrunk, and slipped under the door.

He didn't see Monica in the living room—maybe she was upstairs. As he headed toward the living room, a large fly swooped down and slammed into him. That was weird—other bugs usually avoided him, not knowing what to make of a tiny human. Then another fly was soaring right toward him—its big greenish eyes and long wingspan growing larger and larger until, at the last moment, Scott ducked out of the way.

But more flies were coming from under the door and through a space in the window, and they all zeroed in on Scott, attacking him. He was able to fight them off, of course—he was much stronger than a single fly—but there were so many, already dozens, poking at him, gnawing on him. He swatted them away, but there were too many of them, and it was impossible to get the upper hand. Were they attracted to him because of his sewer odor, the way flies swarmed dog poop on the street? It didn't seem that way—they were unusually aggressive, as if they wanted to kill him.

"Scott, welcome back."

Monica was in front of him, near the kitchen—she must've come up from the basement. She was human-sized, but wearing a helmet that looked very similar, if not identical, to Scott's.

"Looks like you might be like one of the cats I killed as a kid," she said. "I mean, with nine lives. Well, doesn't matter how many lives you've had, you're down to your last one now."

More flies were swarming Scott now, making it difficult for him to see. He tried to activate the Pym gas, to grow big again, but the flies were blocking his hands.

"Oh my god, this works—even better than I hoped!" Monica said. "Wait till I use it on humans! Okay, let's try this…."

Several flies bit into Scott's suit, catching hold with a grip strong enough to lift him off the ground. They flew him around the room, zipping toward the window, then cutting back through the kitchen, and then back toward the dining room. Finally they brought him back into the hallway, hovering in front of Monica.

"This is like the ultimate video game," Monica said. "But it's even better because there's no need for a controller—it's in my mind."

Then Scott heard Cassie's voice: "Daddy!"

Was he imagining her voice? It was hard to see with all the flies blocking his eyes. Every fly in the neighborhood had to be storming into the house.

"Well, this is an unexpected surprise," Monica said. "My favorite kidnapping victim is here to join the party. Welcome, Miss Lang!"

"Daddy, are you here?"

Monica looked back at Cassie, distracted for a moment, and the flies let up. Yes, Cassie was here—man, Tony had done a great job babysitting.

Monica grabbed Cassie and held a gun to her head. Cassie had panic in her eyes, but managed to stay calm.

"Looks like you should've stayed in the sewer where you belong," Monica said.

She didn't realize that the flies had let go. Scott was already charging toward her, still at his ant size. He leapt into the air and easily swatted the gun out of her hand.

"You can't stop me now," Monica said. "I'm more powerful than you are."

"Oh, really?" Scott punched Monica in the face, sending her tumbling backwards. "Could've fooled me."

The flies were attacking Scott again, trying to latch on to him.

"Air power always wins a war," Monica said.

The flies lifted Scott up again, and swirled him around the room. The buzzing was so loud and furious it didn't even sound insect-like anymore.

Then Scott heard Cassie screaming for help. He remembered his promise to her, that everything would be okay. He gathered the strength to fight off a few of the flies, and he activated the HUD.

He had experimented at times with altering the suit's technology to communicate with insects other than ants. One time he'd actually successfully communicated with flies. It required altering the frequency of the command-probe sensor—a difficult task when he was alone, calm in a room. There was no way he could do it while he was being carried around the house by a swarm of flies.

As Cassie screamed, "No, don't!" Scott had an idea. He could try to tap into Monica's device, and use his own helmet as a transmitter. It would be sort of like stealing your neighbor's Wi-Fi.

The flies smashed him against the window, and then flew back in the other direction. Scott managed to shut down the communication software of his helmet, but leave it in "active" mode. And sure enough, it worked.

The flies that were holding him stopped in midair in the middle of the living room. They zeroed in on Monica just as she was about to shoot Cassie in the head. Scott issued his "attack" command, and he and the flies zoomed toward Monica.

"Incoming!" Scott shouted, startling Monica.

Monica's eyes opened wide in shock as Scott grabbed her helmet, yanked it off her head, and tossed it across the room.

Monica lay on the floor, barely conscious—no longer controlling the flies. They backed off from Scott, swarming near the windows. Scott, still ant-sized, easily flipped Monica around onto her stomach. Then he grabbed a dish towel and tied her hands together firmly behind her back.

Scott reverted to human size and hugged Cassie.

"Are you okay?" he said. "What're you doing here?"

Cassie was cringing. "Um, Dad, why do you smell so bad?"

"Long story," he said. "Why did Tony let you leave? How did you know I was here?"

"Um," she said, "that's a long story, too, but I think I figured out what happened to the ants."

She explained that she thought she might have destabilized something in the ant-communication technology, when it tried to function with her brain.

Scott glanced at Monica—she was on her side, unconscious— then did a scan of the Ant-Man suit's software, seeing the results appear on a holographic display. Sure enough, there was an abnormality in the communication circuit.

"Wow, maybe you're right," Scott said. "That's how it happened. Monica had nothing to do with it."

"So how do you fix it? I thought maybe you have to keep it open now, like a portal."

"No, I think it's the opposite," Scott said. "I have to fix the software, then send a new signal."

"You sure that'll work?" Cassie asked.

"No," Scott said, "but there's only one way to find out."

Scott shrunk to ant-size, and then summoned the ants in the area. Ants crawled out of the walls; came from under the front door, the back door, and the basement door. Some were healthy; others were clearly infected with the fungus.

"Cassie, come to the living room with me," Scott said.

He took the remote-control device from Monica's purse. Though he was less than half an inch tall, he easily threw the device over to Cassie.

She caught it. "What're you doing?" Cassie asked.

"*You're* going to do it," Scott said. "If the ants' brains and immunity were affected by this, then maybe we can jolt them back."

"What do I have to do?"

"Aim that thing at me and activate it."

"How do I do that?"

"There must be a switch or a lever. If you figured out how to use my suit, you can figure this out—"

Cassie figured it out.

Scott felt the jolt again, but this time the ant suit wasn't immobilized. More important, the ants that had appeared to be suffering from the fungus immediately started to show drastic improvement. They walked around normally, not zombie-like.

"It worked!" Cassie said.

Scott returned to his normal size.

Monica was partway out of the kitchen now, squirming on the floor with her arms still tied behind her back.

"You're making a mistake, a big mistake," she said, "using your technology like this. What does it get you? You're a criminal, you love money. Work with me. We can be partners."

Then Scott noticed something strange happening—the flies and the ants were targeting Monica. It was a combined ground and aerial assault: the ants, maybe hundreds of them now, attacked her body, biting her, while flies assaulted her from above. More flies and ants entered the house, targeting Monica, as if they instinctively knew she was their greatest enemy, and they had to fight her off.

"Looks like there's been some collateral damage," Scott said.

Monica tried to say something, but there were flies and ants all over her face, and she couldn't speak. Scott put on his street clothes over his Ant-Man suit, and then he and Cassie left the house.

TWENTY

IT'S TOTALLY viral, Dad."

"The ant fungus?"

"No, YouTube. You have over a million views already."

Scott sighed in relief. He had already seen the four-second clip of himself as Ant-Man, emerging from the sewer; it seemed like the whole world had. It was Sunday night, and he and Cassie were at their apartment. The zombie fungus had been curtailed dramatically in one day, confusing scientists who hadn't been able to determine how or why the fungus had started spreading in the first place.

Ant-Man was the big hero. Ironically the viral video had helped him—after the news media had picked it up, he was credited with apprehending Monica Rappaccini, the woman responsible for four murders and implicated in the nonfatal shooting of Roger Shelly, a federal marshal.

Scott had given Carlos the scoop on Monica Rappaccini, which garnered Carlos lots of kudos with his superiors at the FBI. Scott told Carlos that he'd been at the house with Monica when Ant-Man had showed up and saved him. He had a feeling that Carlos didn't quite believe the story, but Carlos was glad that the situation had been resolved. He didn't force the issue.

One complication: When she was apprehended, Monica had revealed to the Feds that Scott was Ant-Man. Scott had expected this to lead to a rush of interest from reporters and curiosity seekers, and he thought he might even have to move to a higher-security building. But so far—aside from comments from old friends on his Facebook page such as "Ha!" and "Congrats!" and "I always knew you were hiding something"—no one seemed to care all that much. He got interview requests from a couple of obscure blogs, but it wasn't exactly like *60 Minutes* was rushing over to do a feature on him. From now on he'd have to be extra careful guarding the Ant-Man technology, but he couldn't help feeling a little, well, silly for putting so much energy over the years into keeping his secret.

He didn't feel any ego blow, though. He preferred to be low key, incognito. The lack of attention and hoopla felt like a gift.

Later, Cassie was in her room when Scott received a text from Tony Stark:

> Great video of you online bro. The ladies will love that one

Scott smiled, texted back:

> Look who's talking, the winner of the babysitter of the year award

Tony came back with:

My bad, but even when I mess up I wind up helping
out, doing something heroic. Guess I just have the gift

In the morning, Cassie came out for breakfast in a short skirt
and a tight top.

"You're going to school dressed like that?" Scott asked.

"It's normal," Cassie said.

"Whatever," Scott said. "I won't judge."

Cassie had a few bites of cereal then said, "Actually, I'm going
out with Tucker after school."

"That's nice," Scott said.

"You don't mind?"

"No, I just want you to be happy," Scott said. "You're getting
older now, I get that. You don't have to tell me about every boy you
hang out with, either. You're entitled to some privacy."

"Wow," Cassie said. "Thanks, Dad."

"You can still call me Daddy," Scott said. "*That* I like."

"Thanks, Daddy." Cassie smiled. "Do you want me to remove
that tracking app?"

"No, it's okay," Scott said. "I don't mind you knowing where I
am at all times. I actually kind of like that."

Cassie left for school.

A little while later, Scott headed to work. It was a perfect spring
day—eighty degrees, no clouds. It was pleasant to walk along the
tree-lined Upper East Side street, past all of the busy, happy ants—
not having to worry, for a change, whether somebody was going to
try to kill him.

On the subway headed downtown, an attractive woman with

short red hair was riding next to Scott. She half-smiled at one point, so Scott had a feeling she was attracted to him.

With all of his bad luck with dating recently, Scott was hesitant to try to strike up a conversation with her. But then again, he didn't want to let a couple of bad experiences tarnish him. He was eager to get his life back to normal.

"Hey, I'm Scott. Can I ask you a question?"

"Sure," she said, smiling. She seemed happy he'd spoken to her.

"How do you feel about ants?" he asked.

"Ants?" She sounded confused.

"Yeah, you know—the most important insect on Earth. They're so awesome, right?"

Scott knew her reaction would determine whether things in his life were truly back to normal.

She just stared at first, maybe confused. Then she sneered and said, "Wow, what a freak," and moved to the other end of the subway car.

Yep, normal.

Acknowledgments

It started where many great things start—at a dive bar in Brooklyn. Big shout out to the entire Marvel team, especially Stuart Moore, Axel Alonso, Jeff Youngquist, and Sarah Brunstad. Being immersed in the world of Ant-Man has been quite a thrill ride, and certainly a highlight of my career. Also big thanks to my parents, for always encouraging me, and booksellers, librarians and readers, for making this all possible.

DEADPOOL: PAWS
By Stefan Petrucha

COMING SOON

PAWS

CHAPTER ONE

SO HERE I am falling off a tall building and...wait.

WHERE THE #$%@ ARE THE PICTURES?

Now I have to deal with this? What is this, anyway—a really, really long caption? Come on! Comics are supposed to be totally in-your-face, in-the-moment, like TV, or...like TV! Get with the program. A picture's worth a thousand turds. Like, if I just *say* red, it's not as good as *seeing* red, is it? Don't get me wrong, I'm all for the chitty-chitty-chit-chat—they call me the Merc with a Mouth for a reason—but enough's enough. Like William Burroughs said, "Language is a virus from outer space."

Okay, yeah, he was a morphine addict, and there's no such thing as a naked free lunch, but still.

I know some of you out there already have smartass questions like, if pictures are so hot, what about backstory? Exposition? How do you do that stuff? Okay, maybe you do need a curt sentence or two, but any writer worth his salt tosses that into the dialogue, like:

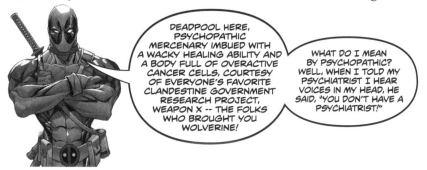

DEADPOOL HERE, PSYCHOPATHIC MERCENARY IMBUED WITH A WACKY HEALING ABILITY AND A BODY FULL OF OVERACTIVE CANCER CELLS, COURTESY OF EVERYONE'S FAVORITE CLANDESTINE GOVERNMENT RESEARCH PROJECT, WEAPON X -- THE FOLKS WHO BROUGHT YOU WOLVERINE!

WHAT DO I MEAN BY PSYCHOPATHIC? WELL, WHEN I TOLD MY PSYCHIATRIST I HEAR VOICES IN MY HEAD, HE SAID, "YOU DON'T HAVE A PSYCHIATRIST!"

None of that *Meanwhile, back at the ranch crap*. If you see a full-page splash of a bank vault, you don't assume the action's taking place in a convenience store, right?

So what's with all the verbiage?

Oh, wait. I get it. Book. It's a book. They really still make these things? Damn.

Okay, I got this. Just a little thrown. As I said, I likes me the talk

I know you do.

By the byway, meet my inner dialogue. If this was a comic, you'd be seeing that in a special-purpose yellow caption. As it is, we're going with that boldface thing, apparently.

Works for me.

Let's get this party started.

And italics for Inner Voice #2. Great. Just shut up for now and let me get on with the story already.

The sleek steel and glass of a Manhattan skyscraper warp into a haze as I careen along its chic frontage. Not being one of those flying types, or even a swinger like Spider-Man, I'm, well…plummeting. I'm flipping and flopping like a fish out of water. More specifically, a fish out of water that's been tossed out a window. I look for something in this big bad blur I can grab onto, anything to try to at least slow my fall, but there's nada No flagpoles, no ledges, no gargoyles—just smooth sailing, first pavement on the right and on until mourning.

Things may look bad, but I've fallen lots. I've fallen down buildings; I've fallen into mine shafts, criminal lairs, alien motherships, candy factories, women's bedrooms—you name it. I've fallen asleep, fallen in love, fallen in debt, fallen to pieces, but I've never, ever, fallen to my death. I have fallen to *other* people's deaths, but that usually involves better aim.

Here's the kicker, though: I'm not alone. I'm carrying the cutest Dalmatian puppy you ever did see. I just snatched this wee fellow from the fancy-pants penthouse way, way back up there. Things didn't go quite as planned, and boy is he going wee now.

I see what you did there.

Oh, aren't you clever.

His name's Kip, judging from the gold tag on his diamond-studded collar. But at this rate, it's going to be Spot when we hit bottom. Under other circumstances, like if he'd eaten a bunch of Cub Scouts and planned to go back for seconds, that might not bother me. Not that I don't enjoy killing, but Kip here hasn't done anything to deserve a premature demise.

So you like the little guy?

No way! He's cute, but cuteness is for lesser beings. I'm the hardened-heart type, keeping the warm fuzzies at bay. That means no man/dog bonding. But...he is so sweet with the rushing air currents pushing his vibrating eyelids wide open like that!

Ahem. That said, I am thinking—purely as a matter of principle, mind you—about how to keep him alive. I did see an online video last week about a puppy that survived a nineteen-story drop.

Sure you didn't imagine it?

Maybe, but it sounded good, especially the part about terminal velocity, where the upward push of wind resistance matches gravity's downward pull, blah-blah-blah. A small mammal like Kip here reaches terminal velocity much sooner than a big guy like me.

Which means...holding onto him should slow me down, right?

Wrong.

Since I'm still picking up speed, I'll give you that one. Kip's stuck with *my* terminal velocity. I can't have that, so I look into his wide, dark, terrified eyes.

"Time you were on your own, little fellow!" I chuck him upward. "Fly free, Kip! Fly free!"

Now that he's on his own, he'll be fine for sure, just like the video. Or was it a cat? I seem to remember a cat. And it was playing piano. Cat, dog, parakeet…what's the difference, really?

I continue to obey the laws of physics. Cumulous clouds spin above me like cream whipping in a blender. Mmm. Whipped cream. I'd grab a little nosh after I land, but the updraft carrying that oh-so-special city stench is ruining my appetite. The ground must be getting pretty close. I should probably look down, just to judge my distance to the pavement, maybe try to slow myself by bouncing against the wall or something.

Pavement, oh, pavement? Where are you?

There you are!

SPLAT!

I mentioned the healing thing, right? You know how when Wolverine, that bad-attitude guy from the X-Men, gets shot or cut, the wound heals all by itself? I'm like that, only…more so. Unless I'm dunked in acid, or completely disintegrated, I grow back. Okay, yeah, most of the super crowd returns from the dead so often they should build a shuttle, but they at least have the *potential* to bite the big one. When one of them comes back, it takes a bunch of convoluted logic—or at most, a reboot.

Me, I'm effectively immortal. No matter how badly I get hurt, everything eventually grows back, cancer and all. Did I mention I have cancer? It's what made me sign up for the Weapon X experiment in the first place. Weapon X was run by the Canadian government, btw. Figured it might be a cure. Instead, the cancer cells regenerate, too, leaving me with a body full of lesions and a head full of dreams.

Or was the word they used *delusions*?

Anyway, missing limb? A few hours, and it grows back. Cracked, flattened skull? Maybe a day or two. Sure, the brain being one of your more crucial organs, I sometimes wake up a little more confused than usual, speaking French, thinking I'm with the Bolshoi ballet or whatnot, but bottom line? Despite what they say about death and taxes, I can't die, and I don't pay taxes.

Doesn't sound too bad, I guess, until it's *your* bones that are broken, your insides spilling out like an overturned Olive Garden garbage can. The problem is I still *feel* every wound, every time. I could go on and on about the throbbing, stabbing agony that's coursing through my each and every neuron at this very moment, but I'm saving that for my next book, *You Think That Hurts?* For now, I'll close on the subject by quoting President Ronald Reagan—who, shortly after taking a bullet, was heard to quip, "Ow! Ow! Ow!"

It does beat the alternative, meaning death. Take the two guys I landed on. You haven't even met them, and they're already no longer with us. Most people think I'm heartless (and gross, smelly, etc.), but I feel pretty bad about the hotdog vendor. The stockbroker? Not so much, though I am impressed with his Patek Philippe wristwatch. It's still working even after I landed on it. Hey, he's not using it, and I've got just enough intact fingers to…

WHAM!

Kip lands in the pulpy center of my cracked chest, making a sound like a wet whoopee cushion. He's all startled, like, what was that? Otherwise, he's no worse for wear. The little guy yips and scampers off. Good for him. Sucks for me.

Nabbing that mongrel is the whole reason I'm here in the first place. Now I have to wait in agony until my body heals, then figure out how to find a puppy in the streets of Manhattan.

Is that a song? A puppy in the streets of Manhattan?

Nah. You're probably thinking about The Muppets Take Manhattan.

By the way, this whole scene? Perfect example of the advantages comics have over prose. It would've been much easier with pictures. Two vertical panels and some motion lines, maybe a quick reaction shot from the hotdog vendor and the stockbroker as they wonder why they're suddenly in shade, and we're done. Half a page, tops. And the slam when I hit? Much more visceral.

Oh, where will all those fools with their "book" learning be in our new post-literate world? Bwah-hah-hah!

Meanwhile, back at the story...

Yeah, yeah. Don't push me.

Before I can cry, "Here, Fido!" I find myself blessed with a visit from above. From the penthouse, not Heaven. Geez. The newcomer lands in front of me, not with an egregious splat or thud, but with the soothing, gentle rush of mech-armor jets. Why, it's none other than the wacky bodyguard who tossed me out of the penthouse in the first place. Never dawned on him I'd be fast enough to snatch up Kip as I went. Should've seen the look on his face.

I don't know if this guy's actually big and mean, or if it's just that high-tech suit he's wearing, but he nails his entrance. The snazzy final blast from his boot-jets whooshes along the sidewalk, sending the cart's still-steaming foot-longs rolling into the street. But that cool *vrt-vrt* noise he makes when he moves spoils it. Totally trademarked by Stark Industries. You can't just order armor like that from Amazon, so I figure he's sporting a black-market knockoff from the PR of China that his boss bought on eBay. Damn Internet. Doesn't anyone just carry automatic weapons anymore?

Iron Joe *vrts* a little closer. The suit does that thing where a missile launcher emerges from his forearm. Don't ask me how it's supposed to work. Unless the suit's made of something like Vibranium, which can absorb vibrations, the recoil on that thing should yank his whole arm off in the other direction.

But he doesn't fire yet. His helmet clicks back, showing me a broken-nosed face with a few miles on it. I can see it in his steely eyes: This man's street-smart, and he may even have been around the block once or twice. He's no hot-shot wannabe out to prove himself. Probably has some combat experience that earned him the penthouse gig. I almost respect him.

Until he opens his mouth.

"Don't know how you survived the fall, and I don't care. Hand over the dog, or I'll decimate you!"

I laugh. "You're gonna destroy a tenth of me?"

His head twists in a how-dare-you way. "What'd you say to me?"

"Decimate, tin man, means to destroy a tenth of something. Don't believe me? That suit must have Internet. Google it. I'll wait."

"Freaking grammar Nazi." He raises the forearm bearing what I'm guessing is a smoothbore 37mm cannon. "I mean I'm gonna blow you up, okay?"

"Okay, but it's not a grammar issue, it's about semantics, as in..."

He nudges me with the barrel—which, given my current state, hurts. "Where's the mutt?"

When he notices I'm lying on a gore pile too big to belong to only me, his face gets all sad. "You didn't...land on him, did you?"

I'd no idea I could actually *feel* my pancreas until he pushes that barrel under me like it's a shovel and uses it to lift me for a peek. "Agh! Cold! Really cold! He's not under there! He ran off! He ran off!"

Relieved, the guard *vrts* his head up and presses a button on his forearm.

From his armor, a sultry synthetic female voice I wish I could hook up with announces, "Dog whistle activated."

The parts of my neck that usually let it move are shattered, so I can't change my point of view, but I hear puppy nails scrabbling along the cement behind me.

Vrt-man gets a smug smile, like he knew all along everything'd turn out fine.

"Kip, you little pain! There you are! C'mere, you flea-bitten dirtbag!"

His words are gruff, but there's a fondness in his voice that tells me he really cares about the hairy thing. Gives me a pang. Could be the pancreas again, but part of me wants to hallucinate a boy-and-his-dog montage with me as the boy—complete with stick, ball, and potty training. Now is not the time.

The bodyguard's not going to want to hear it, but there's something I really should tell him.

"Buddy?"

"Shut up." The scrabbling pup-nails get louder. "Here, boy!"

"What's your name, pal? Look at me down here. I'm good as dead. Might as well tell me that much."

He rolls his eyes, but finding the dog's got him feeling warm, so he gives in. "Bernardo."

Behind me, I hear quick, adorable puppy breaths and a lolling puppy tongue slapping the puppy sides of a puppy snout.

"Bernardo, *mi amigo, por favor*, listen very carefully. I know Kip's cute, I know it's your job to protect him, but you do *not* want to pick up that dog."

Before I can go into detail, I get a view of puppy junk and butt as Kip sails over my face and into Bernardo's waiting metal-composite arms.

"Here you are, you little meat sack!"

"Sure, it *looks* like a puppy, but trust me it's really…"

The dog licks his face. Bernardo laughs, probably remembering a happy day from his childhood that never really happened.

"Hey, settle down, you!"

Then the Dalmatian licks get a little harder. "No, really. Settle down! Kip!"

"Put him down, B. Trust me."

"I'll put *you* down."

The tongue moves faster. The dry, sandpaper feel gets coarser. It doesn't hurt enough to stop a rough guy like Bernie, but I can see from his eyes that he's starting to wonder what's going on. Rather than deal with the strangeness, he turns the anger my way.

"Who the hell are you, anyway? What kind of freak breaks in past a million-dollar security system just to swipe a kid's…"

And then the cute little tongue tears away its first chunk of Bernardo's skin, exposing the tendon and muscle beneath. Surprised—wouldn't you be?—B screams. Instinct makes him want to touch the wound to see how bad it is, but he can't because he's holding Kip in both hands. Teeny Kip, who's now gnawing a gory cheek in his mouth like it's a chew toy.

The welling pain racing his shock, Bernardo gets all nasty. All bets off, he holds up Kip like a football and uses his armor's augmented strength to chuck the mutt as fast and as far as he can. But the furry ball hits the sidewalk just right. Kip rolls, black and white, black and white, like a riddle, for half a block. As he goes, though, he also grows—and grows and grows, until his body's snowballing size mucks with the momentum and stops him short.

Then his body...how do I describe this? Well, it unfurls, sort of like a plant opening up its leaves or a bird unfolding its wings, but more accurately like a mutant monster that's growing, changing color and shape, expanding in seconds to a height of, oh, I dunno. It's not like I've got a ruler handy, so let's call it...forty feet?

Yeah, I'd say forty feet. Give or take.

And then the puppy-no-more cries out, its voice booming like something else that booms. Like, maybe what they used to call a boombox. Sure, a boombox, but much boomier. You know, like thunder. Yeah, like really loud rolling thunder:

"I am GOOM! Thing from the Planet X!"

Cheek-less Bernardo's eyes go wide. I'm disappointed. I thought the man had street-smarts, but he loses a little flesh and suddenly he's some lame desk jockey who's never seen a giant monster before. He's easy prey, too busy staring to realize he should be running.

Me? My body may be broken, but with my heart and soul nestled safely in the burgundy mud puddle that is me, I yell to him: "Hey, Bernardo? 'Nardo, buddy?"

"What? WHAT?"

"Told you."

Continued in

DEADPOOL: PAWS

Available August 2015

X-MEN: DAYS OF FUTURE PAST prose novel
Written by ALEX IRVINE
Adapted from the graphic novel by CHRIS CLAREMONT & JOHN BYRNE
In a dark and dangerous post-apocalyptic future, the mutant-hunting killing machines known as the Sentinels rule America with an iron fist. Almost all mutants, super heroes and villains have been exterminated. Only a handful remain to fight against their oppressive robotic overseers — and most of those are powerless, locked in mutant concentration camps. Now, Kate Pryde must travel back in time and warn the present-day X-Men of the coming danger — and hopefully prevent this horrible future from ever taking place!
Experience the classic, genre-defining X-Men event like never before in this new adaptation!
ISBN: 978-0-7851-8975-6

MARVEL SUPER HEROES SECRET WARS prose novel
Written by ALEX IRVINE
Adapted from the graphic novel by JIM SHOOTER, MIKE ZECK & BOB LAYTON
The fate of the entire Marvel Universe hangs in the balance as Earth's mightiest heroes face their greatest challenge! Summoned across the stars by the mysterious and unbelievably powerful Beyonder, the Avengers, Spider-Man, the Fantastic Four and the X-Men are set against their deadliest foes on the mysterious planet known as Battleworld — with the winner promised the ultimate prize. But as battle lines are drawn, new alliances are forged and old enemies clash, one among them is not willing to settle for anything less than godhood. Can even the heroes' combined might prevent Dr. Doom from becoming the most powerful being in the universe?
ISBN: 978-0-7851-9100-1

**GUARDIANS OF THE GALAXY: ROCKET RACCOON AND GROOT —
STEAL THE GALAXY!** original prose novel
Written by DAN ABNETT
Marvel's first original prose novel, featuring the stars of Guardians of the Galaxy! These are not the Avengers or the Fantastic Four — in fact, they're barely even famous — but Rocket Raccoon and the faithful Groot are the baddest heroes in the cosmos, and they're on the run across the Marvel Universe! During a spaceport brawl, the infamous pair rescues an android Recorder from a pack of alien Badoons, Everyone in the galaxy, however, including the ruthless Kree Empire and the stalwart Nova Corps, seems to want that Recorder, who's about as sane as a sandwich with no mustard. Join Rocket and Groot on a free-for-all
across the stars while they try to save all of existence-again!
ISBN: 978-0-7851-8977-0

AVENGERS: EVERYBODY WANTS TO RULE THE WORLD original prose novel
Written by DAN ABNETT
Just in time for Marvel's Avengers: Age of Ultron: an all-new, original prose novel by the New York Times-bestselling author of Rocket Raccoon and Groot: Steal the Galaxy! and Guardians 3000! The Mighty Avengers face an array of their greatest foes — all at once! In Berlin, Captain America battles the forces of Hydra. In the Savage Land, Hawkeye and the Black Widow attempt to foil A.I.M. In Washington, Iron Man fights to stop Ultron. In Siberia, Thor takes on an entire army. And in Mangapore, Bruce Banner and Nick Fury battle the High Evolutionary. Only one thing is certain: This isn't a coincidence. But what larger, deadlier threat lies behind these simultaneous attacks on Earth?
ISBN: 978-0-7851-9300-5